THAI

SENSATIONS

THAI

SENSATIONS

Sherry Brydson
from the Bangkok Garden Restaurant

Macmillan Canada
Toronto

Canadian Cataloguing in Publication Data

Brydson, Sherry, date.
  Thai sensations

ISBN 0-7715-7322-7
1. Cookery, Thai.   I. Title.

TX724.5.T5B7 1995   641.59593   C95-930382-0

1 2 3 4 5 MP 99 98 97 96 95

Cover and interior design by Gillian Tsintziras
Cover photo by Doug Bradshaw
Food stylist: Kate Bush
Interior photos by Richard Picton
Food stylist: Claire Stancer

Macmillan Canada wishes to thank the Canada Council, the Ontario Ministry of Culture and Communications and the Ontario Arts Council for supporting its publishing program.

Macmillan Canada
A Division of Canada Publishing Corporation
Toronto, Ontario, Canada

Printed in Canada

CONTENTS

FOREWORD

I went to live in Bangkok in 1974. I was a journalist, an editor for Allied Newspapers, the Bangkok Post's group of publications. I lived in Thailand for three years, and I never tasted a dish of Thai food I didn't like.

It was through writing a weekly cookery column that I gained a wide knowledge of Thai food, its ingredients and its history. Almost as soon as my column appeared in the *Bangkok World*, people began calling or writing me to share some special dish or piece of cookery knowledge with me. After three idyllic years in Thailand, during which I was able to travel extensively throughout the country for both business and pleasure, my husband and I returned to Canada. I fully expected to continue working as a journalist—I had been one for 12 years at that point.

But I missed the hustle and bustle on the streets, the colourful disarray of the markets, the constant stimulation of a life lived largely out of doors—and the food!

Finding Western food bland, I put Tabasco sauce on everything. I cooked Thai and spicy Middle Eastern food almost exclusively. I craved the powerful taste and creamy texture of durian so much that I dreamed of it for two months. I missed noodles: soupy noodles and stir-fried noodles and the crispy Mee Grob.

I wanted to maintain a connection with Thailand, and I thought importing and selling some of the beautifully crafted Thai goods I had enjoyed in Bangkok was the answer. I imported hand-painted blue and white porcelain, elaborate fabrics, lacquerware and the intricate and varied handicrafts of the Hilltribes.

I turned my home into a showroom where I would offer Thai lunch and an opportunity for prospective buyers to see how nice the items looked in a home setting. In no time, however, the food was upstaging the products. Our customers and professional advisors were unanimous: "You really should open a restaurant." The rest is history.

Together with partner Barb Elson and Eastern Accents Manager Marie Santorelli, I found an enormous building at 18 Elm Street. It was a wreck, but we knew we could renovate the ground floor into exactly the Thai restaurant we wanted.

During the construction phase, we continued to serve Thai lunches at our offices, using the meals not just as a way of entertaining potential customers or educating suppliers but also as a way of testing the market. There are many thousands of delightful Thai dishes. How on earth does one go about constructing a menu that will remain faithful to the principles of Thai dining while appealing to the Toronto market? Choosing the menu for Bangkok Garden turned out to be one of the most difficult tasks I've undertaken. Our potential customers, suppliers, financiers, families and other well-wishers helped us to shape our first menu.

Six months before the restaurant opened, we were joined by manager Pichai Makmanee, who began assembling his staff of Thai cooks. The upper ranks of his staff have remained virtually unchanged since the restaurant opened in 1982, a tribute to his leadership and dedication to the principles of fine Thai dining. Khun Pichai now owns and manages his own Thai restaurant (Manee Thai) as does our original chef, Prakrith Supsiri (Thai Orchid).

Little did I suspect when I started out as a copywriter "on the rim" at the Canadian Press in the late sixties that I would end up as a restaurateur! I don't miss my former career—this one's too exciting—but after all these years it has been fun to stop talking about Thai food for a while and sit down at a typewriter to put this cookbook together for you. This book is a result of nearly 15 years of cooking Thai food in Toronto, of 12 years of running an award-winning restaurant, of answering customers' queries, of providing recipes for members of the press and of sharing the joys of Thai customs, culture and most of all Thai cuisine with Bangkok Garden's thousands of customers and admirers.

This book makes no attempt to be complete or comprehensive; it arises out of our experience at Bangkok Garden. Recipes were chosen because people have asked for them; many have appeared in similar form in newspapers and magazines throughout North America. Members of the Toronto culinary press have been most supportive of Bangkok Garden and I would like to thank them for encouraging us to develop our recipes for home use.

The superb illustrations in the book's interior are the work of Richard Picton, whose enthusiasm for the material gave us an important lift during the frantic final months. I'm sure Richard's inspirational photographs will galvanize you into a burst of kitchen and shopping activity. Food stylist Claire Stancer provided unparalleled sensitivity in helping Richard bring out the best in the food. Thanks also to Chef Eaw for cooking, carving the garnishes and providing us with a Thai perspective during the photo shoot.

Many others contributed generously to this cookbook: Sujitra Pornprasitt, who tested many of these recipes, created some of them and who shared volumes of Thai culinary lore with me; Chef Lek Vejamont, who tested dozens of the recipes for me; Mary Lou Santos, who typed the manuscript more times than either of us wants to count, while offering valuable suggestions and stick-handling management of the office as well; Tricia Moore and Rebecca Reguly who kept track of the festivals and the files, took care of the press and made terrific suggestions for the graphics; Marcus Elson who supplied computer support; family members Barbara and Tara Elson, Paul MacRae and Gaye Sihin who performed errands, washed up, chased after ingredients at all hours, ate odd meals and looked after Duncan, Cameron and HollyAnne.

All of the recipes in this book are, or have appeared, on the menu at Bangkok Garden and are presented as prepared by our team of Thai cooks led by Chef

"Mom" Payoong Klinproong: Choop Amornsophon, Ariya Chunthahut, Limtoeum Iv, Chawee Sangkapichi, Weerapol (Byrd) Sukcharoen, William Thetsombandith, Olan Vejamont, Uraiwan (Lek) Vejamont, Prayoon (Eaw) Wooldridge, Vilayphone Xayaphone.

Chances are, if you're looking to make these dishes at home, you are looking forward to the pleasures of shopping for the ingredients as much as to the pleasures of preparing them and serving them to your guests. All these recipes have been tested with ingredients we bought at retail from shops in Toronto. Oriental, East Indian and West Indian markets and even supermarkets carry most of the items you'll need for cooking Thai food at home. With the popularity of Southeast Asian cooking as well as the influx of Southeast Asian immigrants to North America, it is possible for you to assemble these ingredients in any cosmopolitan North American city. In order to guide you through the intricacies of a Thai ingredient list, I have devised two explanatory chapters that I hope you'll find useful.

Together with Bangkok Garden Chef, Payoong Klinproong, and her staff of skilled Thai cooks, I am proud to present *Thai Sensations* to you.

Bangkok Garden Restaurant

Since its opening in 1982, Bangkok Garden has become North America's premiere Thai restaurant and has won international recognition as one of Toronto's top ten restaurants.

The Garden is a two-storey oasis of tropical greenery, decorated with teak and brass accents. A gently flowing river with its school of fish is guarded by Naga, a protective dragon-serpent. Thai bronze statuary and original paintings, teak temple-bell light fixtures, pagoda-topped side stands and hand-painted blue and white porcelain tableware and jardinieres grace the dining room. At the entrance is a spectacular display of classical Thai dance masks. Our Spirit House is a Bangkok-style miniature Thai temple; daily offerings of food, water, flowers and incense keep our spirit family happy.

In keeping with Thai cultural tradition, the restaurant was opened by Thai monks who chanted blessings before becoming the restaurant's first customers.

In **The Brass Flamingo**, the restaurant's cozy street-level bar, Thai street noodles are served during lunch time on weekdays to a large and appreciative audience.

Bangkok Garden's team of award-winning chefs has participated in the Escoffier Society's prestigious Salon Culinaire, and has been reviewed and cited by every major communications medium in Toronto, as well as many international publications. Bangkok Garden's Awards include:

1994 - "Canada's 100 Best Restaurants Award," *Restaurant Guide: 100 Best Restaurants of Canada*

- Recommended by *Toronto Life Magazine*, "Best 400 Restaurants"

- The Award of Excellence "a Founding Member of" The Distinguished Restaurants of North America (DiRoNa)

- Reader's Voice Award - Favourite Thai Restaurant, Toronto *Sun*

- Patron's Pick - Best Restaurant in Downtown Toronto (combined ratings of food, service, decor) *Restaurant Guide*, 1994 Patron's Pick

1992 - Member's Choice Award, Coupon program: Entertainment '92

1985, 1987, 1988, 1989 - Neptune Award, "For excellence in seafood merchandising," Canadian Seafood Advisory Council

1985, 1986, 1987, 1988, 1990 - enRoute Award, "Readers have selected Bangkok

Garden as one of their favourite 100 Canadian restaurants in *enRoute* magazine's annual Great Canadian Dining Contest"

1985, 1986, 1987, 1988, 1989 - *Travel Holiday Magazine* Award for Dining Distinction

1982 - Best Restaurant Award or The Toronto *Sun* Good Value Eating Award (food, service, decor), Toronto *Sun*/Percy Rowe

Bangkok Garden Restaurant
18 Elm Street
Toronto, ON M5G 1G7
Tel: 416 977-6748
Fax: 416 977-8280

CHAPTER ONE
HISTORY OF THAI CUISINE

Thai is unquestionably one of the world's great cuisines.

In its bold statements of colour and texture, its subtle inflections of contrasting and complementary flavours and its cunning little culinary twists—a slice of crisp-fried shallot atop a sweet and salty dessert, a spicy meat mixture on a tart slice of fresh fruit—Thai cuisine is easily one of the most complex in the world. Difficult to master, it is immediately appreciated by lovers of dining experience and adventure.

The play of sensations on the palate, the warm rush of a different flavour making itself known after each bite, the high drama of surviving a hot chilli rush followed by the sweet relief of chilled watermelon, so perfectly sliced that even the feel of the fruit on the tongue is pleasurable—all this and more is needed to describe the delights of Thai dining.

THE FIVE TASTE PRINCIPLE

Thai cuisine is based on the "five taste" principle, balancing, blending and incorporating the five principal tastes of sweet, hot, sour, salty and bitter. The bitter taste is found in very few foods, and that taste centre is usually stimulated by the cup of tea or coffee we enjoy at the end of a meal. Tastes within a dish may be balanced for all these sensations, though one taste is usually emphasized.

The taste buds are expected to come to attention at the beginning of the meal and the trick in Thai dining is to choose dishes that continue to startle, amaze, tickle and delight the taste buds until they have been thoroughly stimulated.

A well-chosen Thai meal will include a dish that stimulates each of the taste centres, and the sense of well-being that comes at the end of a Thai meal comes as much from satisfied taste buds as from a full tummy.

The Thai meal centres around a plate of steamed rice and should include a gaeng juut (clear soup), a steamed dish, a fried or stir-fried dish, a yum (salad) and a curry or a bowl of nam prik (a fiery hot dip).

These dishes are not served as courses, but all at once, or as they are prepared, and diners explore the meal with a small helping of each dish in turn, with rice in between, enjoying the play of different tastes and textures on the tongue and palate.

One Thai meal is enough to convince anyone who appreciates good food that here is a cuisine worth exploring. The deeper you plunge into its origins and history, the more you're likely to find. The harder your taste buds work, the more subtleties of spicing and flavouring they'll discover at the heart of a traditional dish. This is hardly surprising since the composition of a Thai dish is the culmination of two millennia of recorded history, the last eight centuries of which have been spent in the present location.

THE INFLUENCE OF GEOGRAPHY

The T'ai tribe originally inhabited the border areas of Southern China in the mountain valleys of Yunnan Province. They began migrating south as early as the first century AD. A Thai-Chinese force captured Hanoi in AD 863 and a substantial southward migration followed. Another major migration took place in the 13th century when the Mongols under the legendary Kublai Khan were terrorizing China. In 1238 the independent kingdom of Sukho Thai Siam (Dawn of Happiness) was formed.

The migrants who arrived in Thailand 800 years ago found themselves in what was to become known as "the rice bowl of Asia." The land was flat and fertile, irrigated by broad, flowing rivers whose annual floods provided rich alluvial soil perfect for the cultivation of rice and all manner of vegetables. The rivers also provided extensive transportation systems, while the annual monsoon rains served to fill the rice paddies with the water necessary for the young plants to grow.

"We have fish in the waters, and rice in the fields. Whoever wants to trade, trades, and the faces of the people shine bright with happiness." This famous passage from an inscription in 1344 by King Ramkamhaeng, creator of present-day Thai script, is today a folk saying meaning "everything's right with the world." Nobody is going to starve in Thailand, where every waterway yields a rich harvest of fish and where a papaya plant grows from seed to fruit in six months flat.

Small wonder that this happy kingdom, situated on a flat plain in Asia's rice bowl, should be regarded enviously by neighbouring countries with aspirations to empire. Because it lies in the middle of a crossroads in Southeast Asia, Thailand has been occupied by various Asian empires which swept back and forth across Southeast Asia as the fortunes of their ruling families rose and fell.

Over the last millennium, the Burmese, Annamese, Cambodians (Khmer) and even an Indian empire have at one time or another held political sway over Thailand's central plains. Through it all the smiling Thai, supreme diplomats that they are, have tolerated their occupiers' diplomats and forces while holding fast to their beliefs, their royal family, their religion, their language, their culture. Being practical, they also helped themselves to any part of the occupier's culture that had merit. Some intermarriage occurred as a dish or a cooking method or an exotic spice was incorporated into the cuisine. A curry originally included in a banquet or festival for diplomatic reasons might adapt well to local ingredients and Thai presentation. The roasted seeds, nutmeg and mace in Red Curry Paste are undoubtedly legacies of Moghul and Burmese occupations, to cite just one example.

Local conditions count for a lot, of course. The climate is hot and steamy, which encourages quick cooking by methods that don't spread the heat around. Even today, many Thai kitchens are out of doors, possibly underneath the house if it is on stilts, in a separate building or, if attached to the house, as far away from the living quarters as possible. Any cooking method that requires an intense but localised heat is used. Consequently over the centuries, Thai cooking methods have changed little, with stewing, stir-frying, steaming, deep-frying and other stove-top methods predominating. Barbecuing is another popular cookery form, for the same reasons.

The subtle flavourings of Thai food depend upon a masterful combination of ingredients both local and imported. The lemony-peppery flavours of lemon grass, krachai root, kha root, the leaf and peel of the wild lime (makrood) locate Thai cuisine firmly in the Southeast Asian heartland. Chilli peppers, introduced into Thai cuisine by Portuguese traders in the 16th century, have a taste—and a fire—that is identifiably Thai.

THE PRINCIPAL INGREDIENTS

Garlic, shallots, the roots and leaves of the coriander plant, tamarind, three varieties of local basil, citrus fruits, ginger, galanga, the fruits of the pepper vine, mint, pandanus, jasmine, and certain man-made sauces such as fish sauce and the fermented shrimp paste called kapi are other essentials of Thai cuisine that spring from the country itself.

Chinese influence on Thai cuisine has been limited for centuries by geography; very little could get past the formidable mountains to the north, although some Chinese influence arrived with an influx of Chinese Ming dynasty potters in the 17th century. Thai cuisine was left untouched by the traditions of Chinese cuisine even though at the end of the last century, a Chinese merchant class established itself in Bangkok. Chinese cuisine has remained separate, and popular Chinese spices like star anise and ingredients such as oyster and soya sauce are not main players in Thai dishes.

Fish and seafood abound in Thailand, from the smallest freshwater stream or canal to the rich waters of the Gulf of Siam. Fish and seafood are eaten fresh, dried or made into fish sauce or kapi. Fish sauce, made from salting layers of fish in a crock and clarifying the resulting liquid, is a sine qua non of Thai cuisine. Many refer to it as "Thai salt" as it is normally used instead of salt. Though it smells potent in the bottle, once it is added to a dish it imparts only a subtle, salty richness with none of the fishy flavour one might expect.

Kapi, made by fermenting shrimps in the sun, then pounding them to a paste and halting the fermentation process with salt (which also acts as a preservative), is a more powerful ingredient, which, when used in small quantities, will enrich and elevate flavour without giving the dish an overly fishy taste. In certain other dishes where the salty, fishy flavour of the kapi is desired, larger quantities are blended with chillies, garlic, coconut milk and fruits or vegetables for those incomparable Thai nam prik—sauces or dips eaten with rice, vegetables and fried fish.

The principal meats in Thai cookery are poultry—chicken, goose, duck—and pork. Beef in former times used to come exclusively from water buffalo, a tough and somewhat tasteless meat. Now some beef cattle are raised in Thailand, but the animals do not take well to the climate; some beef is also imported; both types are expensive. As a result, most Thai beef dishes are water buffalo—either chopped, marinated or stewed.

Pigs, on the other hand, fare superbly in the Thai climate, producing the finest, tenderest, sweetest pork imaginable. Wiener schnitzel and other European veal dishes served by Bangkok restaurants are usually made with local pork—and it is so tender, few notice the substitution.

Goats are raised by the Muslim minorities, but these are relative newcomers to Thailand and goat meat does not feature in Thai cooking except in a few Muslim curries and satay, which migrated north from Malaysia and Indonesia about 150 years ago.

The use of dried seeds, roots and barks as flavourings comes partly from Thailand's stint as an outpost of a 15th century Moghul empire and partly from the generations of Muslim traders who have wandered all over Southeast Asia, carrying with them the dried spices to make their native dishes.

Curious and inventive Thai cooks, seeing the value of such flavourings as coriander seed, cumin, cinnamon, cloves, nutmeg, dried turmeric, cardamom and curry leaf, have incorporated them into some dishes we now regard as Thai classics. These spices also appear in Muslim-style and Muslim-inspired dishes such as Gang Massaman and Gang Garee.

POLITICS AND CUISINE

For the past eight centuries, against a backdrop of war and occupation, in spite of trade contact with Muslim and Portuguese traders, French and Dutch diplomats, and, in this century, two devastating world wars, which brought the country swiftly and sometimes reluctantly into the world community—in spite of all this, the country has remained virtually intact since the Thai migration of the 13th century.

On three sides, the integrity of its borders can be explained by natural phenomena: the mountains of Southern China to the north, the mountains of Burma to the northwest, the Andaman Ocean and the Gulf of Siam to the south and along the Isthmus.

There are no real natural barriers between the eastern borders of Thailand and the lands of Cambodia and Vietnam, formerly Annam, but both these countries have been separate racial and cultural entities for at least as long as Thailand has; it is their separate cultures that keep them separate today as in centuries gone by.

A glance at Thai history shows that the three dynasties of royal families that ruled the country as gods until the present king's grandfather declared the nation a constitutional monarchy in 1932 have been responsible for holding fast the customs, traditions and even language.

The Royal Court of Siam is a huge community, which includes the residences of the king and the royal family and their retainers, government offices, judicial offices, the military and the Royal Chapel. All things flow from the royal court. It has always been the source of Thai culture and religion and it was in the court kitchens that Thai cuisine was created, nurtured and preserved.

In 1767 the Thai capital of Ayuthaya was a city of over 1 million ruling the greatest rice-producing nation in the world. The court was at a pinnacle of cultural development: the arts flourished, royal scribes had filled the library with priceless manuscripts, the great Throne Hall was a wonder of gold leaf and inlaid and carved wood; nearby a pavilion of gold leaf and black lacquer displayed the ultimate in the decorative arts. Stone temples stood everywhere, many housing priceless Buddha images of gold and gems.

During a tragic war with Burma, which is said to have started with a dispute over which king was the owner of an auspicious white elephant captured on the border of the two countries, the Burmese invaded the country and laid siege to the glorious capital, leaving it a charred ruin.

By destroying the royal court, the Burmese had in effect brought down the entire civilization. The resulting loss of books, records, artifacts and architecturally significant buildings was a cultural tragedy comparable to the loss of the library at Alexandria, which was burned in the third century AD during a Roman civil war.

But the Burmese did not occupy the country and the shattered remnants of Thai society retreated south along the Chao Phraya River to what is now Bangkok to regroup and to begin to piece together Thai civilization and society.

The Court Nourishes the Faith

Thai civilization might have ended right there had the people not fallen back on their traditional source of strength, the royal court. In short order the Chakri dynasty was founded, and the first Chakri ascended the throne as King Rama I in 1782. The nine kings of this present dynasty have had as their task not only ruling a country but also of rebuilding, encouraging and preserving the ancient Thai culture. Each king is known for his special encouragement of one or two elements in society—religion, education, legislation, medicine, the arts and so on.

Thai cuisine scarcely skipped a beat as a new court established itself in Bangkok, and an 1809 record of a meal offered by King Rama I to 2,000 monks during the dedication of the Emerald Buddha Temple indicates that Thai cuisine was one of the first elements of the culture to recover from the shattering of the Ayuthaya era.

The royal family and gentlemen of the court are invited to take part in offering food to the monks. After detailing an extensive Thai menu, most of which is still commonly eaten today, the king directs court attendants to fetch from the Inner Court a soup of Chinese origin and from the Muslim officials of the Harbour Department portions of Indian rice and curry. All of which indicates that Thai cuisine was kept separate and distinct even in a society still struggling to recover from a fatal blow dealt within living memory.

Perhaps the preservation of Thai cuisine is also due to the importance of food in the Buddhist religion. Food is offered to Buddhist monks as part of every Thai ceremony. King Rama I knew that his most important task was to rebuild the religion, to build temples and to re-record lost manuscripts, teachings and legends.

The king also directed that traditional festivals be observed and here was an occasion to bring out traditional dishes prepared in special ways. By keeping alive the institution of the monarchy and through it the Buddhist religion with its attendant rituals and festivals, Thailand was assured that its culture—and its cuisine—would survive.

Eating for Thais has always been a pleasure and an entertainment, and the court has always been a lively source of the culinary arts. King Chulalongkorn (1868-1910), Thailand's great modernizer, was fond of giving parties and fancy-dress balls for which he did, or directed, the cooking himself. He was also fond of giving cooking demonstrations as a form of court entertainment, peppering his instructions with witty puns or comments on the history of a dish or ingredient.

In bringing his nation into the modern era, King Chulalongkorn also caused a liberalization of the society. Culinary traditions, long held as closely guarded secrets within the court, began to filter out to the people at large. Members of the royal family wrote cookbooks or taught the royal art of vegetable carving to members of the public. To this day, most of the noted authorities on Thai cuisine are members of the royal family or their protégés.

Thai culinary arts are supported by an enthusiastic public. The Thais are rivalled only by the French in their passion for all things culinary. Mention to a Thai friend that you're going for a drive in the country; he'll immediately recommend a bakery, noodle shop or fruit orchard you must visit along the way. Thais departing even on very short journeys pack a picnic—even if they are planning to stop at the famous noodle shop along the way! From the day the mango trees first begin to blossom, speculation begins on what sort of mango season it will be this year. Everyone exchanges opinions on the best place to buy whatever fruit is in season, which markets carry the best curry paste, which regions produce the best nam prik, and which ingredients go into the proper preparation of certain curries.

HOW TO CHOOSE A THAI MENU

First-time customers to our restaurant often worry that they do not know how to order a Thai meal. You may feel the same way trying to plan a home-cooked meal from a recipe book. Relax. "There are no rules in Thai dining," we tell our guests. "Feel free to choose whatever appeals to you, and to eat it (with rice) in any order you choose." The only requirement—and it may prove tricky to follow—is that the meal chosen must stimulate the five principal taste centres on the palate.

In order to help you with your menu planning, I have identified the principal taste in each recipe. Use this as a guide for putting together between three and five dishes that, together with steamed rice, will make up your menu.

Start as you would for any menu, with the principal dish you want to serve. Let's say it is Red Curry of Chicken. Look up the recipe: you'll see its principal taste is hot. Note also that it is rich, containing coconut milk. Now look for a salad. Most Thai yum or salad dishes are hot and sour. It's OK to have two "hots" but now you need to find some dishes that are predominantly sweet, salty or bitter. (Don't worry *too* much about the bitter. You can take care of that with coffee and in garnishes if necessary.)

You have a rich hot curry and a light hot and sour salad. Now you need something sweet and salty and not too rich. How about a stir-fried vegetable dish like Stir-Fried Butternut Squash with Egg? Or a stir-fried Oriental vegetable like Jade Greens?

If you'd like to serve a soup, any of the gaeng juut will go nicely with the meal. Don't consider a soup with coconut milk, as this would clash with the curry. And you can eliminate the hot and sour soups (tom yum) as they are too similar to the yum salads.

Let's assume you'll be ending your meal with fresh fruit and tea or coffee. Your menu now looks like this:

	Principal Taste:
Red Curry of Chicken	*Hot, Salty*
Citronella Shrimp Salad	*Hot, Sour*
Stir-Fried Jade Greens	*Salty*
Baby Corn Soup	*Slightly Salty*
Steamed Thai Rice	*Neutral*
Fresh Fruit	*Sweet*
Tea, Coffee	*Bitter*

You'll have now satisfied all the taste centres. Now review the menu for other important considerations. Is there a variety of colours? textures? temperatures? You might want to make changes to get more crunch. Sometimes you can achieve this by adding more garnishes, or even a plate of crispy raw vegetables.

Finally, is this enough food? It's a good meal, but you might want to add another dish, possibly a noodle dish or an appetiser. You could add something deep-fried, crisp-fried or steamed, in any of the taste sensations.

If you use the Five Taste Principle as a guide, I'm confident you will be able to structure many wonderful Thai menus from the recipes in this book. To get you started, here are a few more suggestions.

Dinner Party for Six:	Principal Taste:
Coconut Seafood Mousse	*Hot, Salty*
Stuffed Cucumber Soup	*Slightly Salty*
The Royal Barge	*Hot, Sour*
Emerald Curry of Duck	*Sweet, Hot, Salty*
Stir-Fried Bamboo Shoots	*Sweet, Salty*
Steamed Rice	*Neutral*
Thai Banana Fritters	*Sweet*
Tea, Coffee	*Bitter*

Lunch for Two:

Coconut Chicken Soup	*Sweet, Hot*
Green Papaya Salad	*Hot, Sour*
Sweet and Salty Air-Dried Beef	*Sweet, Salty*
Steamed Sticky Rice	*Neutral*
Fresh Fruit	*Sweet*
Tea, Coffee	*Bitter*

Light Lunch or Dinner:

Fresh Spring Rolls	*Nearly Neutral*
Elephant Ear Salad	*Sour*
Stir-Fried Scallops with Basil	*Sweet, Salty*
Steamed Rice	*Neutral*
Ice Cold Watermelon	*Sweet*
Tea, Coffee	*Bitter*

Children's Menu:

Thai Spring Rolls	*Children tend to*
Stuffed Chicken Wings	*favour dishes that*
Bean Thread Chicken Noodle Soup	*are sweet, salty and*
or Anytime Noodles, wet, with beef	*sour, in about that*
Kids' Curry	*order.*
Steamed Rice	
Banana Fritters	

Thai Banquet:

Appetisers:

Pork Pearls	*Salty*
Curried Mussels on the Half Shell	*Hot*

Soup:

Fisherman's Catch	*Hot, Sour*

Principal Dishes:

Emerald Curry of Beef	*Sweet, Hot, Salty*
Crispy Noodles	*Sweet, Sour*
Toasted Cashews with Chicken	*Salty, Sweet, Hot*
Steamed Rice	*Neutral*

Desserts:

Coconut Pumpkin Custard	*Sweet*
Mock Pomegranate Seeds	*Sweet*
Fresh Fruit	*Sweet*
Tea and Coffee	*Bitter*

TO CALCULATE PORTIONS

Portion size depends on a number of factors, including the number of diners, the number of dishes to be served and your best guess as to how hungry your guests are likely to be. I have generally found that North Americans like to eat more meat than Thais, and have adjusted the recipes accordingly.

Assuming you're serving 4-6 people, use these quantities as a rough guide.

Meat/poultry/fish: allow 3.5 oz/100 g per person in curries and stir-fries; 2 oz/50 g per person in salads, rice and noodle dishes; less in soups and appetisers.

Noodles (uncooked weight): for dried noodles, 2 oz/50 g per person. For fresh noodles, 3.5 oz/100 g per person.

Rice: 1/2-1 cup (125-250 mL) uncooked rice per person. This works out to 1-2 cups (250-500 mL) cooked rice. Remember, you need a lot of rice if you're serving curries and other spicy dishes.

Vegetables: 1/2-1 cup (125-250 mL) uncooked vegetables per person.

Fish: a whole fish weighing approximately 2 lb/1 kg serves 4-6 people.

All of these portions assume you'll be serving at least three dishes (for example, a curry, a stir-fried vegetable, a steamed fish), plus rice.

TABLE MANNERS

Thai food is eaten with a fork and spoon, and has been for some generations. The spoon is the business implement, scooping up the rice and all that good sauce, and the fork is used in the left hand to push food onto the spoon.

Many foods are eaten with the fingers, including lightly steamed vegetables dipped in the sauces called nam prik. Sticky or glutinous rice is also eaten with the fingers. It's fun to gather up a bite-sized ball of sticky rice, dip it in your nam prik and pop it straight into your mouth. Sticky rice is even served with the fingers— it's much easier to break off a chunk from the main serving dish than to try to get it up on a spoon or fork.

Thai food is not eaten with chopsticks, although they are often used as cooking implements. Foods of Chinese origin such as noodle soups are eaten with a Chinese soup spoon and a pair of chopsticks, and the Chinese soup spoon is the soup spoon of choice at the Thai table.

A Thai meal tends to be served all at once, or as the dishes are prepared. There may be several serving dishes on the table at once. Each diner is served a portion of rice. Diners then help themselves to small amounts of one or possibly two dishes, not a large amount at any time and seldom more than two items at a time. To enjoy a Thai meal it is important not to allow the flavours to run together—after all, a great deal of preparation time went into achieving just the right balance in each dish. No one wants to spoil that balance by running two dishes together.

A Thai meal is a leisurely affair, meandering along with pleasant company and conversation; a Thai in a hurry will grab a bowl of noodles at a corner street stall, or eat a plate of stir-fried rice in the market. Because it is so delicious, we serve some of these street or market foods at Bangkok Garden even though they would not be found on the Thai table at home or in a full-service restaurant. Som Tam (Green Papaya Salad) and Laab Issan (Northern-Style Chopped Beef) are examples of dishes you'd be more likely to find in the market than at home, but they are so delicious and so typically Thai that I feel they merit inclusion both in our menu and in this book.

CHAPTER TWO
THE THAI KITCHEN

Cooking in the tropics is a simpler affair than cooking in temperate climates. Preparation time may be longer, but cooking time is generally short in order to conserve fuel and to avoid heating up the house, the kitchen—and the cook.

Thai dishes are seldom baked: ovens are expensive and hot. Steaming in a many-layered stovetop steamer is much more energy efficient and, incidentally, a superior way to cook rice. Thai dishes are also boiled, braised, deep-fried, stir-fried and stewed on top of a stove or a single fuel-efficient charcoal brazier. Many favourite Thai dishes are also barbecued, though it is more common for barbecued dishes to be eaten outside the home—let someone else suffer the heat!

UTENSILS

Good Thai food does not require a battery of complicated and expensive equipment. You can produce a good Thai meal in any moderately well-equipped kitchen that contains some heavy-bottomed pans and some good sharp knives.

Apart from what you would already have in your kitchen, you'll find the following equipment useful:

A heavy wok with spatula for stir-frying and a slotted or basket-weave spatula for deep-frying;
A multi-layered steamer, or sung, with a reservoir at the bottom and a close-fitting lid for steaming rice, fish, vegetables and hors d'oeuvres;
A mortar and pestle for pounding curry pastes, bruising chillies and garlic or reducing spice mixtures to a paste. Choose a mortar with very high sides—it keeps the food inside while you're pounding. Even if you plan to do most of your grinding and pounding in a blender or coffee grinder, you'll need to do a final pounding in the mortar to release essential oils, which are not released no matter how finely the ingredients are cut with a blade. Mortars come in many sizes. The one in daily use in my kitchen stands about 15 cm (6 in) high and has a capacity of about 2 cups (500 mL).

A WORD ABOUT HEAT

"There are only two important settings for your burner," grins Bangkok Garden Chef "Mom" Payoong Klinproong, "high, and off." This is only a very slight exaggeration. Most Thai food is fried, steamed, seared or boiled quickly at a very high heat. Much time is spent in preparation, and everything is cut into bite-sized pieces, thus reducing the need for lengthy cooking time.

If you're getting ready to cook Thai food for the first time, get used to the "high" setting on your stove-top burners. Remember, all Thai recipes were developed originally on small individual charcoal firepots, which deliver an intense, direct heat. The art of Thai cooking is to capture and retain all of that heat in your cooking utensil, thereby preventing it from overheating you and the space around you. (You can see why it's important to use heavy-bottomed pans!)

Thai cooking is mostly done *à la minute*, and—except for curries—should not be made ahead and re-heated. Do all your preparation ahead of time, but don't actually cook a dish until you're ready to serve it. Perhaps for this reason, or perhaps because the weather is usually so warm, Thais don't consider it important that a dish be delivered steaming hot to the table. As long as it's warm, serving temperature isn't important.

In fact, some dishes are meant to be eaten at room temperature. Laab with sticky rice, Festival Noodles and Yum—salads combining cooked and raw ingredients—are just a few examples of dishes that are never eaten steaming hot.

MISCELLANEOUS ESSENTIALS

Coconut Milk and Coconut Cream

Many people believe the liquid inside a mature brown coconut is the coconut milk referred to in tropical recipes. This is a logical deduction, but incorrect. The thin liquid inside a mature coconut, usually called coconut water, is regarded as a beverage. The silky, sinfully rich coconut milk and cream used in soups, curries and desserts is

Thai: Naam gati, Hua gati

obtained by grating the flesh of mature or "old" coconuts, soaking it in hot water, then squeezing the pulp to extract the oil-rich coconut liquid. When cool, the liquid will separate into a liquid milk and a thicker or even solid cream, which, just like dairy cream, has a very high oil content. For recipes to make fresh coconut milk or coconut cream, see page 100.

Although the finest results in taste and texture are to be obtained from fresh coconut milk and cream, canned coconut milk is quite acceptable. Several excellent Thai brands are widely available in Oriental and Caribbean shops, as well as in some supermarkets.

When purchasing coconut milk, be sure to read the ingredient declaration carefully: some brands contain sugar and should not be used under any circumstances, even when you are intending to sweeten the dish anyway. Sweetened coconut milk or cream is for Pina Colada only and should never find its way from the bar into your kitchen.

To separate the cream and the milk, refrigerate the cans for a few hours before opening. The cream will solidify while the milk remains liquid, enabling you to pour out the liquid and to spoon out the cream.

Fermented Soya Beans, Fermented Soya Bean Paste

Thai: Tao jeeo
Also called:
Fermented
yellow beans or
Salted soya
beans

Cooked soya beans are fermented for varying lengths of time. The fermentation process is stopped by adding salt just before bottling. It is most commonly sold as beans in brine, though it can also be pureed before canning or bottling. The puree may be any colour from yellow to red-brown to black, depending on the beans, the processing method and other additives. (Watch for those additives! The salt is preservative enough; there's no need to buy a product full of chemicals.)

These beans can be called many things from "Salted Yellow Beans" to "Fermented Beans in Brine," depending on who translated the label at the factory. I buy the ones in glass jars so I can see what I'm getting. I like to see lots of yellow-brown bean halves in a liquid that is dark, but not cloudy.

Fermented soya beans are very salty and should be used sparingly. They give a rich flavour to stir-fried dishes, steamed fish and soups. The Japanese miso paste is a more refined version of the same thing.

Fish Sauce

Fish sauce is sometimes called "Thai salt" because it regularly replaces salt in the Thai kitchen. It is made by mixing fish and salt in large jars, leaving them in the sun for several months, then drawing off and clarifying the liquid that results. The resulting sauce, thin and about the colour of a good clear Orange Pekoe tea, is extremely salty and replaces salt in the cuisines of Thailand, Cambodia and Vietnam. It is also widely used in Indonesia, Malaysia, the Philippines and many regions of China. Ignore the strong smell of this essential ingredient: once it is added to a dish the fishiness somehow disappears, leaving behind a salty richness of flavour.

We use Squid Brand fish sauce, available at most Oriental groceries—Chinese, Vietnamese, Thai, Lao, Filipino. It comes in a glass bottle with a green plastic top and has a large drawing of a squid on the label. When choosing a fish sauce, hold the bottle up to the light—it should be a clear red-brown.

Substitutes: None. Fish sauce is what makes a Thai dish truly Thai and should not be substituted under any circumstances. Fortunately this essential is available in all Oriental food shops, and is becoming a common sight in larger "mainstream" supermarkets. Only in dire emergencies should you contemplate substituting salt, or good quality light soya sauce flavoured with anchovy essence or a little mashed salted anchovy.

Flours

In the Thai kitchen, flours are used mainly in desserts and in batters for deep-frying.

Thai: Nam pla
Ind/Malay:
Ketjap ikan
Vietnamese:
Nguoc mam

Where a main dish has a gravy or thick sauce, thickening is usually achieved by reducing the liquid through rapid cooking. Oyster sauce, fermented bean paste and pounded peanuts also act as thickeners. No Thai cook would create a fresh stir-fry and then make the resulting gravy gummy with the addition of cornstarch (this is one way to tell if you're being served a Thai or a Chinese dish). Only the noodle dish Laad-naa, which is Chinese in origin, relies on cornstarch to make a thick gravy.

In desserts, rice flour, sticky rice flour, mung bean flour and tapioca or cassava flour are the major players. If you're interested in learning to make Thai desserts, it's essential to get to know these flours. Be prepared for some failures as you learn about their peculiarities. As the qualities of these flours differ vastly from brand to brand, it's not really possible to offer reliable advice. Use these recipes as guidelines, be patient and be prepared to experiment until you achieve the results you're looking for.

Cornstarch

Cornstarch, which the British refer to as cornflour, is a pure white and very fine starch refined from the endosperm of the corn. It is not to be confused with corn flour, which is ground from the whole corn kernel and is yellow in colour and considerably grainier than cornstarch.

Cornstarch is used as a thickener and a stabiliser and is particularly good with acid fruits as it is more resistant to breakdown in the presence of acids.

It is not commonly used to thicken gravies, a fact that distinguishes Thai stir-fries from some Chinese dishes.

Rice Flour

The rice flour referred to in this book is made from refined white rice and has excellent thickening properties even though it contains no gluten. It will tend to clump, stick or burn at lower temperatures than other flours. Do not use rice flour in a dish you're intending to boil or simmer more than a few minutes. Dishes thickened with rice flour need to be stirred often to prevent sticking.

Tapioca Flour (Cassava Flour)

Tapioca flour is a pure white highly refined flour processed from the cassava root. The cassava is native to Brazil, but has taken well to the Thai climate and in fact is today one of Thailand's major agricultural exports.

Tapioca flour is especially clear when cooked, but it should never be allowed to boil as it becomes stringy when overcooked. For this reason, it takes some time to get used to cooking with tapioca flour.

Sago Flour

Sago, saku in Thai, is refined from the fruits of sago palm trees. It has exactly the same properties as tapioca and the two flours are used pretty well interchangeably in Thai cooking.

Sticky Rice Flour

Sticky rice flour is made from refined white glutinous rice and is largely called for in desserts. It has a similar action to other rice flours but as the name implies, it is more glutinous when cooked. It holds up well for deep-frying, which ordinary rice flour does not. For obvious reasons, it is sometimes called glutinous rice flour.

Mung Bean Flour

This may also be labelled merely "bean flour." Made from the small green beans commonly used to make bean sprouts, this flour is higher in protein and lower in starch than the other flours. For this reason it is usually recommended for diabetics and others seeking to reduce the amount of simple starches in their diets.

Mung bean flour is very clear when cooked.

Wheat Flour

Wheat flour isn't used much in Thai cooking, for the simple reason that it's a temperate climate grain not readily available in the tropics. Even for batters, sticky rice flour and mung bean flour are more commonly used, although wheat flour can usually be substituted for these with excellent results.

The best wheat flour to use is unbleached white soft. Even this very fine flour is no substitute for the quick-dissolving cornstarch, and won't produce the clear jelly-like result that tapioca flour does in Mock Pomegranate Seeds.

The main use for wheat flour in Thai cuisine is in noodles such as Bah Mee, which Thai cooks purchase already manufactured. And the soft white noodles that form the basis of kanom cheen, or Festival Noodles, are sometimes made of wheat flour instead of the traditional rice flour.

Fresh Chilli Paste

Ind: Sambal oelek

A number of bottled fresh chilli pastes sold commonly in Oriental markets can be quite useful. They can be easily identified by their fresh red colour and the whole seeds, which are quite visible through the jar. The fresh red colour results, unfortunately, from the addition of some sort of sulfite preservative, so read the labels and don't use if you suspect a sulfite allergy.

If you are able to use bottled fresh chilli paste, it can cut down preparation time and eliminates the need for you to sting your fingers every time you need crushed chillies. It's also great in non-Thai dishes or even by itself as a sauce. It is also a quick and easy way to add extra "zap" to any curry or stir-fried dish.

We use a bottled product called Tuong Ot Toi Viet-Nam, a chilli-garlic sauce that keeps well in the fridge and is extremely handy.

Fructose

Throughout this book I specify the sweetening agent in most dishes as "fructose or other sweetener." Sweeteners are essential in Thai cooking and it's important to be able to taste them clearly. But modern palates are jaded and over-stimulated by sucrose, the ordinary white cane sugar we normally think of when the word sugar is mentioned. Sucrose is a natural anaesthetic. It stuns the palate and gradually interferes with the ability to discern other flavours.

After going to the effort of obtaining fresh Thai ingredients, preparing them meticulously and blending the flavours carefully, I would hesitate to toss a palate-stunner into my curries and stir-fries. Fructose, a gentler sugar that sweetens without dulling the palate, is now available in granular form and I use it at home as well as at Bangkok Garden. You can also use other sugars such as honey, corn syrup or maltose to good effect.

Monosodium Glutamate

Monosodium glutamate is the chemical name for a salt that is variously called MSG, Accent, Taste Powder, Ve-tsin, Aji-no-moto and Gourmet Powder. A sodium form of glutamic acid, which was originally extracted from wheat, this chemical occurs naturally in soya sauce. It is sold as white crystals and has no flavour of its own. It has the ability to liven up anything it is added to, by intensifying the flavours. A present-day sine qua non of Chinese cookery, monosodium glutamate has been identified by some health authorities as a possible cause of liver damage, and the United States Food and Drug Administration has banned its use in baby foods. Because of this possible health hazard, we recommend it not be used.

Substitutes: A few drops of lemon or lime juice have the same effect as a teaspoon of monosodium glutamate and present no danger to health. Thai cooks have for centuries relied upon the freshly squeezed juices of limes, lemons and other citrus fruits to enhance the delicate flavours of soups, salads, noodle dishes and curries.

Noodles

Noodles appear in Thai cooking in bewildering variety. It helps to break them down into their main ingredients.

Noodles can be made of rice flour, wheat flour, wheat flour with eggs added, and with mung bean flour.

Woon Sen
Woon Sen are the noodles made with the high-protein, low-starch mung bean flour. (The mung bean is the small green one most commonly used for bean sprouts.) These noodles are sold dried in convenient 50-g bundles. Allow one bundle per person for soups, up to four per person for

Thai: Pong choo rot

main dishes such as Stir-fried Glass Noodles. When cooked, they are perfectly clear, which is why they are often called Glass Noodles. Other names for this noodle are bean thread, vermicelli, cellophane.

Rice noodles

These come in two types, fresh and dried, and in many thicknesses.

Rice noodles that have been dried and rehydrated stand up best to stir-frying, and are used for such dishes as Thai Rice Noodles, or Phad Thai. Use any thickness of dried rice noodle that appeals to you for this dish. They are often called Rice Stick, for some reason.

The same rice noodle is sold in round sheets, and it is this noodle we use to wrap our Fresh Spring Rolls. Many varieties of rice noodles made in Thailand can be found in Oriental food stores with little effort. Erawan, with a picture of a three-headed elephant, seems to be the best brand.

Fresh rice noodles appear in Chinese-style dishes such as noodle soup and the delightfully easy Anytime Noodles, Phad Laad-Naa. Any city with a Chinese community will have a store where you can purchase freshly made rice noodles. Another type of fresh rice noodle is purely Thai. About the size of Japanese soba or Italian spaghettini noodles, they are coiled into "nests" after cooking. For a dish such as Festival Noodles, Kanom Cheen, allow five "nests" per person. These noodles are served at room temperature with a warmed sauce poured over them and a selection of crispy and crunchy garnishes to contrast with the softness of the noodles themselves. Tradition has it that these noodles were part of the Lord Buddha's last meal, which is why they are a favourite at celebrations.

Wheat flour noodles

These are generally Chinese in origin. They may occasionally be used as wrappers for giaw (won ton in Cantonese), which are eaten deep-fried as snacks or boiled in soups. Giaw squares may also be used to make the tiny Thai spring rolls that are such a signature item in Thai cuisine, although rice flour wrappers are usually preferred because they are crispier when fried.

Bah Mee are wheat flour noodles with egg and are yellowish-brown in colour. They are sometimes called Wonton Noodles when sold fresh in Oriental food shops. They can be deep-fried and served with a mild lightly flavoured mixture of vegetables, mushrooms, quail eggs and chicken in a light delicately flavoured sauce.

And noodle vendors offer Bah Mee from their street stalls, poached briefly in boiling water, sprinkled with vegetables, meats and condiments. Patrons of these street stalls may choose to eat them "wet"—that is, covered with soup broth—or "dry," in which case they often take them home wrapped in banana leaves and newspaper.

Oils

Thais once did most of their frying and deep-frying in coconut oil or pork fat; this tradition has almost entirely vanished and Thais now use corn or light vegetable oil for most dishes.

Generally speaking, your Thai dishes will taste best when you use good quality, pure vegetable oil. Choose the lightest oil available. Under no circumstances should you use lard as this will impart a heavy flavour and feel, which will defeat the delicate balance of flavours on which good Thai food depends.

Safflower, peanut and olive oils have strong flavours of their own and should be avoided if possible.

For deep-frying, nothing beats the crispness achieved with canola oil. It's worth looking for this versatile oil, which is now carried in most stores. Canola oil has the added benefit of being one of the lowest in cholesterol.

Coconut oil, used in curries, should not be purchased separately. There's enough coconut oil in the coconut milk and coconut cream, as you'll discover as soon as you begin to stir-fry your curry paste.

Oyster Sauce

This thick brown salt/sweet sauce is made from oysters cooked in soya sauce and brine. Some of the cheaper products are labelled oyster-flavoured sauce and contain few, if any, oysters. Taste it before using, as different brands have

Thai: Namman hoy

differing degrees of sweetness and saltiness. It is used as the basis for the gravy in some stir-fried dishes, blending well with meats, seafood and vegetables. If a Thai dish contains oyster sauce, it's a sure sign of its Chinese origin or influence.

Substitutes: Available worldwide in Chinese and gourmet shops. In an emergency, blend a little sweet, heavy soya sauce with molasses or honey. Another approximation is to thin fermented bean paste with soya sauce and sweeten to taste.

Palm Sugar

Thai: Namtaan beep
Bot: Borassus flabellifer (Palmyra palm)
Hindi: Jaggery

The sap of the coconut palm or sugar palm is boiled down and sold crystallized in cakes or blocks. It has a characteristic flavour all its own and it's worth the effort to locate it in Oriental, Indian or West Indian shops for use in sweet dishes. A key ingredient in the unusual Son-in-law Eggs (Khaay Luuk Khooey).

Substitutes: Soft brown sugar; honey.

Peanuts

Unroasted peanuts are a basic Thai condiment. You can usually find them shelled and skinned and packed in clear plastic bags in Oriental and east Asian stores.

Otherwise, buy peanuts in the shells, available in most supermarkets, and shell and skin them yourself. Do not substitute roasted peanuts as they are too strongly flavoured.

Pound peanuts roughly so that the largest pieces are the size of barley and about half the pieces are the size of coarse salt. Serve in small bowls as a garnish to sprinkle over soups, salads or noodle dishes.

Unroasted pounded peanuts can be used as a secret ingredient to thicken sauces. Make sure no one is allergic to them before tossing them into a dish!

Rice

White Rice
Thais prefer a long-grain rice. Several varieties are grown in Thailand and there is quite an art to choosing the proper

rice at a Bangkok rice dealer. In North America, choose a Texas or California long-grain variety, or buy Thai rice imported in 5, 10 and 25-kg bags, called variously Khaaw Horm, Sweet Rice, Fragrant Rice and Jasmine Rice. Check with your merchant to make sure it's the long-grain variety and not sticky rice, which I'll come to in a minute. Interestingly, rice cooks best when it has had a chance to dry out for about six months. Rice that is very newly harvested will cook up very soft and often too soft for stir-frying as fried rice. Some people like Patna rice but unless it's a Patna from Texas, I find the taste too strong for Thai meals. Rice is a very personal thing.

Sticky Rice—Khaaw Niaw

Sticky rice, or glutinous rice as it is often called, is not, as some people surmise, "regular" rice cooked in some special way. It is a short-grain variety of rice that cooks up harder—and of course stickier—than long-grain varieties. It is often served instead of regular rice as a main-course staple in the northern areas, and is a mainstay of the Lao diet. Sweetened with sugar and coconut milk after cooking, it is a favourite sweet all over Thailand. The flour made from sticky rice is valued for dessert-making because of its glutinous properties. There's really only one way to cook sticky rice, and that is to steam it.

There's really only one way to eat sticky rice, and that is with the fingers.

Roasted Rice Powder

Some recipes in this book, notably yum dishes (salads), call for roasted rice powder as an ingredient or garnish. You can easily make this in a wok.

Heat a clean, dry wok or frying pan until it starts to smoke. Add 2 tablespoons (30 mL) uncooked long-grain rice and stir-fry at high heat, stirring constantly, until rice turns a medium toasty brown.

Remove immediately from pan to stop the roasting process. Allow to cool, then pound in a mortar with a pestle until rice is the consistency of coarsely to finely ground black pepper (some of it will be fine and some will be coarse). Store in a tightly covered jar until ready to use. Roasted rice powder will keep for 6 months or more.

Note: if you don't have a mortar and pestle, put the rice in a strong bag and beat with a rolling pin, bottle or hammer. Young children love to help!

Roasted Rice Powder is also available in the spice section of some Oriental grocery stores.

Salted Turnip

Thai: Hua chaay tao

Also called preserved radish, salted radish and preserved turnip according to the whim of the packager, this is the white root vegetable the Japanese call *daikon*. It starts out as a large elongated white radish with some green tones (it can also be pale green all over). It is packed fresh in salt, and as the salt draws the water out of the cells, the vegetable turns a medium brown and becomes quite flabby.

It is usually diced or shredded fine and used to add body and saltiness to a dish. A favourite addition to rice and noodle soups.

Salted turnip is widely available in small vacuum packs in Oriental food stores.

Shrimp Paste

Thai: Kapi Ind/Malay: Trassi or blachang

This paste is made by pounding very tiny shrimps (and sometimes fish scraps as well) with salt. It can be quite powerful-smelling and is used in small quantities in many Southeast Asian dishes. It is available in most parts of the world, especially in Dutch and Chinese shops. Look for a greyish-pink paste. Don't be put off by the powerful smell.

A small quantity disappears into a dish, leaving behind a richness of flavour with no trace of fishiness. Some Thai dipping sauces have shrimp paste as their principal ingredient and these dishes are extremely pungent and fishy. If you like very strong cheese, you might enjoy one of these dishes.

Substitutes: Buy dried shrimps from an Oriental food shop and pound to a paste, using a little fish sauce and a little vegetable oil as a lubricant. If you're really stuck, try pounded salted anchovies—but don't expect the results to be the same.

Soya Sauce

The basic process for making soya sauce involves fermenting a mixture of salt, cooked soya beans and wheat or barley flour, then extracting the liquid.

Light Soya Sauce should be about the colour of good fish sauce (clear tea), salty and not too strongly flavoured. It should be used for most stir-fried dishes where flavours should be delicate.

Dark Soya Sauce is a heavier version of the same thing, often thickened with flour. Be careful when choosing your dark soya sauce: the Chinese and Japanese types are best. Many types manufactured and sold outside of the Orient are sweetened with caramelised sugar, thickened with flour and adulterated with other substances. They can ruin a dish.

Sweet Soya Sauce is a heavy black soya sauce flavoured with molasses. Use it sparingly for it is very strongly flavoured. A substitute can be made with oyster sauce thinned with light soya sauce and flavoured with sugar or honey. Indonesian sweet soya sauce (ketjap manis) is excellent and is available worldwide in Dutch and other gourmet shops.

Sriracha Sauce

The universal Thai bottled hot sauce, Sriracha originated in a fishing village of the same name about an hour's drive southeast of Bangkok. It is made of hot red chillies, vinegar, salt and sugar and aged in barrels until it becomes a thick red sauce.

It was originally developed for spicing up the fresh, lively seafood caught daily in the Gulf of Siam and delivered still jumping in baskets to small ocean-side restaurants. It is traditionally served with steamed and deep-fried fish and shellfish.

Bottled Sriracha comes in three strengths—mild, medium and hot (look for the rating on the neck of the bottle)—and is available in many Chinese and most Southeast Asian stores.

*Thai: Light: Sii iaw khaaw
Dark: Sii iaw
Sweet: Sii iaw waan
Bot: Glycine max (Glycine soja)*

In larger cities, Sriracha sauce is starting to appear in supermarkets as well. It has become so popular it is now being manufactured in the United States.

Tamarind Puree

Thai: Naam macaam

The large brown pods of a tropical tree are dried and sold in blocks similar to dates. A puree made from soaking these pods in water is used extensively in Thai cooking to lend a rich tangy (sour) flavour to curries, soups and sauces. To make the tamarind puree used in these recipes, soak a block of dried tamarind in an equal quantity of boiling water, to cover. Allow to cool to room temperature, then squeeze through cheesecloth or strain through a sieve. (See also TAMARIND, page 39.)

CHAPTER THREE
FLAVOURS

It's difficult to isolate a single most important factor in getting the flavour of Thai food just right.

As with any cuisine, the perfect taste depends upon a marriage of flavour, intensity, cooking method, quantities used, garnishes and so on.

It's tempting sometimes to substitute one ingredient for another, especially if the ingredient is difficult to obtain from local shops. In order to make your Thai dishes taste just right, it's important not to make substitutions for key ingredients. Once you start substituting celery leaves for fresh coriander, salt for fish sauce or curry powder for curry paste, you've destroyed the balance that is needed for an authentic Thai dish. You may produce something quite tasty—it just won't be Thai food.

WHEN IN DOUBT, LEAVE IT OUT

What to do if you don't have a certain ingredient? It may be better to carry on without it, as long as you have the other ingredients. You can get away with a lot as long as you have the three most essential ingredients in the Thai culinary lexicon: garlic, fish sauce and black pepper.

In this chapter I've tried to answer all the questions we've been asked at Bangkok Garden over the years about the essential flavours that make a dish uniquely Thai.

Basil

There are many kinds of basil around the world, each with its own distinct flavour. The Thai basils go in strength from the strongly flavoured horapha (for chicken curry) to krapow (beef curry, frog's legs) to the mild manglak (soup, fish, vegetables).

Thai:
Bai krapow,
Bai horapha,
Bai manglak

*Bot: Ocinum
basilicum
Ind/Malay:
Selasi
Also called:
Sweet basil,
Holy basil*

Horapha seems to be the nearest to European sweet basil, and is often served raw as a vegetable with sticky rice and nam prik. Krapow leaves are narrower and often tinged with reddish purple; they release their flavour only when cooked. Krapow stalks tend to be purple or tinged with purple. You can get away with using this one for all the dishes in this cookbook. Manglak leaves are slightly hairy and paler green than horapha.

Manglak is sometimes called lemon-scented basil and has a peppery taste somewhat similar to Italian dwarf basil.

Basil has great affinity with tomatoes, eggplant, sweet peppers, fish, chicken, shellfish and dishes containing wine. It is at its best when fresh, becoming stronger and somewhat peppery when dried.

Substitutes: None; available worldwide.

Caraway

Thai: Yeerah

*Bot: Carum
carvi*

The caraway plant is native to Europe, Persia, India, Turkey and North Africa and its seeds are used mostly in German, Austrian and Central European cooking. The seed is small and dark brown with lighter brown stripes and is often confused with cumin—probably because both are called jeera (yeerah) in Thai and Hindi. In curry powder or paste recipes cumin is often mistranslated as caraway. The two are not really interchangeable: caraway has a bitter flavour and should not be used in Thai cooking. Cumin has a more full-bodied, "meaty" flavour.

Cardamom

*Thai: Luuk
grawan (seeds);
Bai grawan
(leaves)*

*Bot: Elattaria
cardamomum
Ind/Malay:
Puarlaka
Hindi: Elachi*

The cardamom plant is a perennial of the ginger family and grows in moist, shaded areas in tropical climates. Its seed pods can be round or elongated, green, brown or bleached white. Inside the pods are tiny, sticky round black seeds.

Ground cardamom is sold worldwide but it does not keep well in this form, and cardamom should be used whole or ground fresh whenever possible. It is used ground in European cakes and pastries, in Turkish coffee, Middle Eastern and Indian curries and pilaus, and whole in pickling spice mixtures, custards and rice puddings. Cardamom goes especially well with peanut-based dishes, and is an essential ingredient in Thai Massaman, or Muslim-style, curry.

Substitutes: None.

Chilli Peppers

Thai: Prik

Bot: Capsicum frutescens

There are many varieties of "hot" chillies grown around the world in varying sizes, colours, shapes and strengths. The only way to test the mettle of a chilli is to taste it: some species (those used for paprika, for example) may look bright red and fierce, but taste sweet and mild. Use of chillies in cooking is largely a matter of personal preference. They can be preserved in brine or vinegar (but this reduces their "hotness"), in oil or in alcohol such as vodka or sherry. They may also be dried and purchased whole, crushed or powdered.

In ascending order of "hotness" the chillies most commonly used in Thai cooking are:

Banana peppers (large and pale green)	*Prik yuak*
Finger-hot green or red chillies	*Prik chee fa*
Yellow chillies	*Prik luang*
Tiny bird chillies (red or green)	*Prik kii nuu*

If you wish to lower the "heat" in a dish calling for chillies, don't make the mistake of thinking you can do it by reducing the *number* of chillies in the dish. The sting and bite of a hot chilli is carried in the volatile oil capsaicin. Milder chillies taste milder because they contain less capsaicin. By using a milder-tasting variety of pepper, you still get the pepper flavour while achieving your objective of lowering the bite. Conversely, to increase the bite of a chilli dish, go for the hotter varieties.

Dried chillies can be crushed and added to a dish for extra kick. To make them hotter still, dry-roast dried chillies before adding them to the dish. And the bite of a fresh chilli is always increased when you bruise it to release its oil of capsaicin.

Bamboo shoot has the ability to intensify the bite of hot dishes. You might like to add it as a vegetable to curries and stir-fries to make them even hotter.

Substitute: For fresh chillies, substitute a chunk of fresh sweet pepper plus crushed dried chillies to taste. Black pepper is not a substitute for chillies, but can be used to add "heat."

Cassia

See Cinnamon.

Bot: Cinnamomum cassia

Thai: Prik pon

Bot: Capsicum family

Cayenne Pepper Powder

A coarse orange-red powder of ground dried hot chillies, cayenne pepper is widely available in Western countries and is used to make dishes "hot."

Substitute: Other powdered chillies, Tabasco sauce, other hot pepper sauces to taste.

Cinnamon

Thai: Ob chuey

Bot: Cinnamomum zeylanicum

In most countries, cinnamon and its close relative cassia are treated as the same plant. True cinnamon is native to Sri Lanka and has a milder flavour than cassia. It is the bark of this small evergreen tree, which is used (in pieces or powdered) almost worldwide. Cinnamon bark is very thin and usually longer in cigarette-sized curled-up rolls, while cassia is much shorter and thicker. For sweet dishes, the milder flavour in cinnamon is preferable, while cassia bark may be used in spiced meats, pickles, pilaus and curries. Cassia buds, which resemble withered cloves, may also be used to impart a strong cinnamon flavour. They may not be used interchangeably with cloves.

Substitutes: None; available worldwide.

Cloves

Thai: Gaan phu

Bot: Eugenia aromatica Ind/Malay: Tjinkeh or chinkeh

Clove trees grow some 10 metres high and flourish only near the sea in tropical areas. Native to Southeast Asia, they are also grown in Zanzibar, Madagascar and the West Indies. The fresh buds are picked before they flower and turn a dark brown colour when dried. Cloves have a powerful, penetrating flavour, and act as both antiseptic and anaesthetic. Oil of cloves is an ancient remedy for toothache. Cloves give flavour to meat and chicken dishes, curries, pickles, ham and spiced wine drinks. In Thailand, cloves are not used widely although they are used in some curry pastes (notably Massaman) and in some Northern and some Chinese-inspired dishes.

Substitutes: Can be found worldwide, but allspice may be substituted.

Coriander

Coriander leaves: The young leaves of this small plant are used as a garnish for Chinese, Japanese, Indian and Southeast Asian dishes. They have a distinctive flavour, which does not appeal to some palates and may be omitted if the pungent flavour of coriander is not liked. Coriander leaves are also found in Mexican, South American and some European cuisines.

Substitutes: None.

Coriander seed is used in curries, pickles, sausages, baking and savoury dishes nearly everywhere in the world. It goes especially well with peanut dishes. It is best stored whole and ground as needed as it loses its flavour rapidly once ground.

Substitutes: None.

Coriander root is pounded for use in many Thai curries and stir-fried dishes. It's one of the lemony/peppery flavours that makes a Thai dish truly Thai. Fresh coriander roots can be successfully frozen for use when needed, so always buy your fresh coriander with roots left on. Wash roots, dry well and store in a plastic bag in the freezer. If your coriander doesn't have roots, and your recipe calls for it, use some of the lower stems.

Hindi: Laoong

Thai: Pak chee

Bot: Coriandrum sativum
Malay: Ketumbar
Hindi: Dhania, kotimli

Also called: Chinese parsley, Japanese parsley, cilantro

Thai: Luuk pak chee

Thai: Rak pak chee

To get best use from a bunch of coriander: Buy it with the roots on. Put in a glass of water and cover the leaves loosely with a plastic bag. Change the water every 2-3 days. The bag acts as a mini greenhouse to keep the leaves fresher. Don't forget to save those roots in the freezer!

Substitutes: No real substitute, although a little parsley root and a slice of lemon peel bears some resemblance to coriander root.

Cumin

Thai: Yeerah
Bot: Cuminum
cyminum
Malay: Djinten
Hindi: Jeera,
Zira

Cumin is grown on the North African coast, Malta, Sicily, the Middle East, India and America. There are two kinds, one that yields a small black seed, and a somewhat more oval-shaped grey one with ridges. Often confused with caraway, fennel and sometimes with fenugreek, it has a completely different flavour from any of these. It has a dominant flavour with none of the bitterness of caraway or the sweetness of fennel. It increases the meaty taste of meat dishes and gives pulse dishes the impression of containing meat. It should be used sparingly for best effect. Used mostly in curry pastes.

Thais generally do not care for the flavour of cumin and when used at all it is very much a background spice. Warning: Toasted cumin seeds are used in red curry paste. There are many Thai cookbooks in print that claim caraway or even fennel can be substituted for cumin. This is just not so. In my view, it is better to omit a spice altogether than to use one that is going to give your Thai dish Indian or Hungarian overtones. If you're cooking with a Thai recipe that calls for caraway or fennel, treat this as an error and substitute cumin.

Substitutes: None. Ground cumin keeps its flavour for relatively long periods of time, and can be found worldwide.

Curry Leaf

Thai: Bai karee

The basic ingredient in Madras curry powder, curry leaf is also used in Muslim, South Indian and Pakistani cooking. Good with goat, beef and chicken curry and also with vegetables, these leaves are essential only in Indian and

Muslim-inspired Thai curries—our Three Pagodas curry, for example. Best when fresh, they can be purchased dried in most Indian shops worldwide.

Substitutes: Madras curry powder to taste, or the fresh leaves of the chilli plant.

Bot: Chalcas koenigii (Murraya koenigii) Ind/Malay: Daon karri Hindi: Katnim, mitha neem Tamil: Karuvepila

Dill

This feathery plant is a member of the parsley family and is most prominent in the cuisines of Scandinavia, Germany, Russia and the Balkans. In Thailand, it is available fresh all year round and is used in Laotian-type dishes, particularly fish dishes.

Substitutes: For the leaves, fennel. For the seed, fennel or caraway—though the result will be somewhat different. Dill seeds are available worldwide, and the plant grows freely in almost any climate.

Thai: Pak chee lao

Bot: Anethum sativum

Fennel

Fennel is another feathery plant similar to dill, and in Thai cooking they may be regarded as the same plant, for they are picked so young—about 6 weeks—that the flavours are almost identical. It has a sweet flavour resembling anise while dill has a more bitter bite. In India, fennel (or anise) seeds are chewed after meals to cleanse the palate and to aid digestion.

In Thailand, young fennel, dill or anise plants are most likely to appear as a garnish.

Substitutes: Dill or anise.

Thai: Pak chee lao

Bot: Foeniculum vulgare

Galanga, Galangal

The root (rhizome) of this plant of the ginger family is pale yellow with pinkish sprouts. It grows in moist areas in tropical conditions and is best known in the Thai dish Gai Tom Kha (sometimes called Tom Yam Gai). It has a flavour all its own, though it vaguely resembles a lemony ginger

Thai: Kha Bot: Alpinia officinarum or Alpinia galanga Indo: Lao Malay: Lang kuas

Sometimes called: Siamese ginger or Lesser ginger

without the bite: astringent rather than peppery. It is an essential ingredient in many curry pastes.

Once an important spice in Europe, it is virtually unknown there today. Galanga was probably introduced to Europe by Marco Polo and the traders who followed him on the Silk Road and kept Europe supplied with this tasty root. It was used widely in the medieval cooking of most trading nations, but began to disappear during the last century. In medieval writing it's usually called Galingale.

Look for it in Chinese shops, dried and sliced. The dried slices can be rehydrated with some success. Be sure to add the soaking water to the dish along with the root slices. Fresh galanga root travels well and you may be lucky enough to locate some in a Southeast Asian grocery. It will keep for many weeks in a cool place particularly if you keep it dry and packed in sand, peat moss or vermiculite.

Substitutes: None. Dried, powdered and labelled laos, Kha is available in gourmet shops and Dutch shops worldwide, but it bears about as much resemblance to the real thing as dried powdered ginger.

Garlic

Thai: Gratiem

Bot: Allium sativum

Garlic, the bulbous, segmented root of a plant of the onion family, needs little introduction. Garlic grown in the tropics is very weak in flavour when compared to garlic grown in temperate climates—so when changing countries, beware! A temperate-climate recipe calling for one clove of garlic may actually need two or three when the shopping is done in Thai markets, and Thais who go abroad should start with very little temperate-climate garlic and add until the dish tastes right.

The recipes in this book call for temperate-climate garlic.

Garlic changes its taste according to how you treat it. The gentler you are with it, such as steaming and baking, the milder the flavour. Garlic that has been sliced or chopped with a sharp knife cooks up milder than garlic that has been smashed with the flat blade of the knife before chopping. Crushing garlic starts an enzyme reaction that actually changes the flavour. This enzyme change also explains why raw garlic tastes so different from cooked.

Although Thais use a lot of garlic in their cooking—even in some desserts—they rarely use it raw.

Garlic Chives

A cousin of the chive, this plant can be easily identified by its flowered head. It is picked when the flower is in the bud stage. It has a strong flavour that goes well with noodles, steamed fish and stir-fried dishes.

Garlic chives are an essential accompaniment served raw, with Thai Rice Noodles and Crispy Noodles.

Substitutes: Leeks, green onions, chives.

Thai: Gweechai

Bot: Allium tuberosum
Ind/Malay: Kutchai
Also called: Onion chives, Onion grass

Ginger

The root (rhizome) of this native Southeast Asian plant is known worldwide as a flavouring for just about anything edible. The ideal "hand" of ginger should be pale tan, smooth-skinned and not too fibrous when cut. It may be used fresh: grated, bruised, shredded or pounded.

Substitutes: None. Fresh ginger root can be found in your local grocery store. Dried ginger root, soaked in warm water for an hour, should only be used in moments of desperation, and dried powdered ginger only in case of nuclear war.

Thai: Khing

Bot: Zingiber officinale
Indo: Djahe
Malay: Halya
Hindi: Udruk

Green Onions

These are simply very young onions picked before they have had a chance to form a bulbous base. Some varieties never form a bulb at all. Best eaten raw as a garnish, they are also good when cooked briefly, as in stir-fried dishes or clear soups.

Substitutes: None; available worldwide.

Thai: Ton hom
Bot: Allium fistulum
Ind/Malay: Bawang muda
Also called: scallions, spring onions, Welsh onion, Japanese bunching onion. Sometimes mistakenly called shallots.

Kha

See Galanga.

Krachai

Thai: Krachai

*Bot: Kaempferia
pandurata
Ind/Malay:
Tumu kuntji*

A strangely shaped yellow-brown root having many fin-
ger-shaped tubers, krachai is unknown in the West and has
no European name. It is used in several soups and curries in
Malaysia and Indonesia. In Thailand, it is always used in
fish curries and Nam Ya and peeled and served as a raw
vegetable with Khao Chae, a chilled rice dish. If you have
a local Thai, Lao, Khmer or Vietnamese grocer, ask if they
have any in the freezer.

Substitutes: None.

Lemon

Thai: Manau

*Bot: Citrus
limon*

Lemon juice can give a dish real zest without adding an
extra flavour, and a few drops can do more for most foods
than monosodium glutamate. Thais prefer the flavour of
limes; in the Thai kitchen lemon is best used as a substitute
for lemon grass and lime leaves.

Substitutes: Lime juice, though this will alter the flavour of
the dish. Never use lemon essence, bottled lemon juice or
other imitations.

Lemon Grass

Thai: Takrai

*Bot:
Cymbopogon
citratus;
C. flexuesus;
C. nardus
Ind/Malay:
Sereh
Also called:
Citronella*

A tallish grass with a slightly bulbous base, lemon grass
smells delightfully lemony when bruised. The stalks are
generally tough, even when quite young. It is featured
prominently in Thai, Ceylonese and other Southeast Asian
cooking. Lemon grass is also cultivated in Africa, South
America and Florida. This aromatic herb is the essential
ingredient in Tom Yam, the Thai national soup. The stems
must be bruised, sliced or pounded in order to release their
flavour.

Lemon grass is now being grown in Florida, California
and other parts of the United States. It travels well and will
keep well in a cool, dry place for many weeks. If you should
come across a plant with some roots on it, plant it and in
about a year you should be able to harvest a crop—it will
"bunch" like onions.

Substitutes: Dried lemon grass, while not as good as fresh, is quite acceptable. Be sure to soak at least 1 hour before using. Add the soaking water to the dish along with the rehydrated lemon grass. Or use a generous strip of lemon peel in place of one stalk lemon grass.

Lime

Used in everything from salads to drinks, the lime is indispensable in Thai cooking, mainly as a souring agent and flavour enhancer. Though its flavour is markedly different from the lemon, the lemon may be substituted when limes are unavailable. For some reason, Thais use the word "lemon" to describe both lemons and limes. When Thais specify lemon juice as an ingredient, they usually mean lime juice. If a Thai recipe calls for lemon juice and you can't check, it's best to assume lime juice is what is meant.

Thai: Manau
Bot: Citrus
aurantifolia
Ind/Malay:
Jeruk nipis,
Limau nipis

Lime, Wild (Makrood)

The double leaf of this wild lime is used in soups, curries, and shredded fine onto sweets and savouries. Along with lemon grass and galanga it is an essential ingredient in the Thai Tom Yum soups. The peel of its knobby green fruit is pounded into curry pastes.

Substitutes: For both leaves and peel, use lime or lemon rind.

Thai: Luuk
makrood
(the fruit)
Bai makrood
(the leaf)

Bot: Citrus
hystrix
Ind/Malay:
Daon jeruk
limau (the leaf),
Jeruk limau
(the fruit)
Also called:
Papeda, Kaffir
Lime, Citrus

Mint

This hardy plant grows virtually anywhere in the world and varieties have tastes ranging from the familiar spearmint (the "toothpaste mint") to lemon, pineapple and apple. Used mostly as a fresh herb garnish in Thai cooking, mint also features in salads (Yum), the popular Laab Issan and some stir-fried dishes. Fresh mint is often used in combination with fresh basil. Dried mint is not an acceptable substitute.

Thai: Saraneh

Bot: Mentha
family

Nutmeg

Thai: Luuk jaan

Bot: Myristica fragrans
Ind/Malay: Pala
Hindi: Jaiphul

The nutmeg tree, a large evergreen, is native to Indonesia and the Philippines, though now grown in other tropical countries. The nutmeg seed is light brown, oval and about the size of a quail's egg. Always use fresh whole nutmeg, grating as much as you need for each dish.

Substitutes: Mace in equal proportions, although it yields a slightly different flavour.

Pandanus Leaf

Thai: Bai toey

Bot: Pandanus odorus
Ind/Malay: Daon pandan
Also called: Screw pine

This fragrant leaf may be as much at home in a flower arrangement or a temple offering as in the kitchen. It is used mainly to wrap fish, bits of chicken or meat for steaming and barbecuing, and for flavouring sweets (kanom chan, for example) and the rice known as khaw man kati in Thai, nasi guri in Malay.

Substitutes: A rough approximation can be achieved with a bay leaf and a stick of cinnamon. Pandanus extract can be found along with the rosewater and jasmine essence in most Oriental and Indian shops.

Pepper

Thai: Prik thai

Bot: Piper nigrum

The pepper vine flourishes in tropical countries with a wet climate or monsoon: India, Thailand, Indonesia, Sri Lanka, Madagascar and Brazil. In their unripe form, little green berries hang in bunches from the vines. Black pepper is harvested green and dried in the sun, whereupon it turns black, with a wrinkled surface.

White pepper is allowed to ripen on the vine until it has turned red, then the outer skins are washed off, leaving a smooth white peppercorn. It has a milder flavour than black pepper and is preferred for use in light soups (gaeng juut).

Black pepper, pounded in a mortar with garlic and fish sauce, is an essential Thai flavour.

Roselle

Native to tropical Asia, this plant has not been in popular use for long. The red flesh surrounding the immature buds is very sour and juicy and is high in pectin content. Alone, it can be used as a souring agent. Sweetened, it is made into drinks, jams and jellies. In Thailand it is served as a sweet drink and served preserved as a dessert. (Thais also use the word "grajiep" for the vegetable okra.)

Its main use is as a substitute for tamarind.

Substitutes: As a souring agent, use tamarind puree or pomegranate juice.

Thai: Grajiep

*Bot: Hibiscus sabdariffa
Also called:
Red or
Jamaican sor-
rel, Hibiscus,
Rosella*

Shallot

The small onion-like bulbs of the shallot can be pink or red in colour and ideally should have a flavour midway between onion and garlic. Note that spring or green onions are sometimes incorrectly called shallots. Essential in curry pastes and stir-fried dishes, and widely incorporated raw into Thai salads. Sliced and deep-fried shallots are also a popular garnish.

Substitutes: Onion, lightly flavoured with garlic.

Thai: Hom daeng

*Bot: Allium ascalonicum
Also called:
Spanish garlic*

Sweet Peppers (Capsicum)

Sweet green and red peppers belong to the chilli family but are larger and have no "bite" to them. Most commonly used as a vegetable.

Thai: Prik yai

*Bot: Capsicum anuum
Also called:
Green (or red)
pepper, Bell or
Bele pepper,
Capsicum,
Pimiento.*

Tamarind

The fruit and pods of this enormous tree found in most tropical areas of the world are dried and will keep almost indefinitely. A juice or puree is obtained by soaking these pods in water and squeezing. It is an important souring agent in Asian, Indian and West Indian dishes. Available

Thai: Macaam piak

Bot:
Tamarindus
indica

dried in most Oriental, Indian and West Indian food shops. Bottled tamarind juice is also sold, though it is very thin.

Substitutes: Lemon juice, lime juice, sour pomegranate or roselle juice.

See TAMARIND PUREE, page 26.

Turmeric

Thai: Khamin

Bot: Curcuma
longa
Hindi: Haldi

Incorrectly called Indian saffron, turmeric is the bright yellow-orange rhizome of a plant of the ginger family. Best known as a colouring agent (it was once used to dye the saffron robes of Buddhist monks and to polish girls' skin), it has an earthy flavour usually associated with curries.

The fresh root can be used to colour the coconut milk used in making yellow rice, and when pounded into a curry paste, give a more delicate flavour than dried powdered turmeric. The powder gives prepared mustards and bottled curry powders their characteristic yellow colour. Fresh turmeric root is also served peeled and raw as a slightly peppery-tasting dipping vegetable with sticky rice and spicy dips.

CHAPTER 4
APPETISERS

The saying "from soup to nuts" would not translate well into Thai. The Thai meal does not really have a set place for appetisers in the Western sense as the first course of a meal. A Western meal starts with a dish designed to whet the appetite and bring the taste buds to attention, and proceeds in a straight line from one course to the next in strictly defined order.

Thais approach a meal with a different sense of the order of things. The various dishes of a Thai meal are served all at once or as they are completed; the central point in the meal is a plate of perfectly prepared white rice. Each dish is carefully chosen to contrast with or to complement the others, in colour, texture, temperature and contribution to the balance of the five tastes—sweet, sour, salty, hot and bitter.

Thais do have snacks, nibbles and food to eat while doing something else. Air-Dried Beef, for example, is a favourite snack for drinkers and card players, who eat the chewy beef with handfuls of roasted peanuts. But as for selecting one dish and serving it in isolation from the others as a "first course," Thais just don't think of doing it.

On the other hand, there's no reason why a Westerner, accustomed to ordering a meal in a certain way, can't select one dish and eat it first as an appetiser. It won't spoil the enjoyment of the meal and it won't offend anyone's principles; it's just another way of doing things. In writing the menu for Bangkok Garden and in choosing the recipes for this section, we looked for dishes that adhered most closely to Western concepts of appetisers. In choosing a Thai meal to prepare from these recipes, please feel free to select any dish in the book you like, and serve *that* first. The following recipes are some of our customers' favourite appetisers.

FRESH SPRING ROLLS
Porpia Sot

These delightful spring rolls, somewhat like a salad wrapped in a thin rice pancake, are served uncooked and at room temperature. Make them large, cut them into serving-sized pieces and serve with sweet plum and Sriracha sauces.

You can tailor these spring rolls to your own taste by adding whatever ingredients appeal to you. Some typical Thai additions might include fresh basil leaves, fresh mint leaves, chillies of various strengths, broccoli stems, julienned and briefly steamed, Chinese cabbage, bamboo shoots, mushrooms, glass noodles and cucumber. You might also try sprouts of various kinds, avocado, tomato, asparagus, Jerusalem artichoke and eggplant. Just make sure everything is cut to a relatively uniform size and that nothing is too runny.

Here's how we make our Fresh Spring Rolls at Bangkok Garden:

Vegetarian

2 oz	bean sprouts	50 g
4	green onions	4
4 tbsp	bean curd (fresh or cooked)	60 mL
8	water chestnuts	8
1	carrot	1
3	eggs, lightly beaten	3
4 tbsp	fresh coriander leaves	60 mL
4	large rice paper crepes	4

Non-Vegetarian
For meat eaters, add one or more of the following:

7 oz	chicken breast, steamed, julienned	200 g
7 oz	shrimp or scallops, steamed	200 g
1	Chinese sausage, julienned	1
7 oz	barbecued pork, shredded	200 g

Remove the roots from the bean sprouts. Keep in a bowl of cold water until ready to use. Cut green onions into 1 1/2-inch (4 cm) lengths. Cut bean curd into small cubes or julienne. Cube water chestnuts. Grate carrot or cut in fine matchsticks.

In skillet, cook eggs into thin omelet. Drain, cool and cut into thin shreds.

RELATIVELY
NEUTRAL

Separate crepes and dip in lukewarm water to soften, drain and lay on clean work surface. They will change colour from clear to white and feel rubbery.

Lay lines of prepared ingredients, along with coriander leaves, and choice of meat if desired, on one-third of each wrapper. Roll up tightly, tucking ends in as you roll. Cover with a damp cloth until ready to serve because crepe will dry out and harden within 10 minutes in the open air. To serve, cut each roll into five bite-sized pieces. Serve on a bed of lettuce, garnish with fresh raw vegetables and serve with sweet and hot sauces to taste. **Makes 20 pieces.**

THAI SPRING ROLLS
Porpia Tod

Spring rolls can be found on menus from Seoul to Manila and have been adopted with great success by leading-edge North American chefs.

The rolls consist of a chopped filling of meats, vegetables and/or seafoods rolled up in a cylindrical pastry (pasta) wrapper and crispy deep-fried in vegetable oil.

The preparation of ingredients for this dish, as in so many others, is Thai art. Notice that most of the principal filling ingredients—eggs, mushrooms, crabmeat, bean sprouts, noodles and onions—are the same size and shape. Although you're not likely to spot this visually since it's wrapped up tightly in a crisp cover, your tongue will appreciate this subtle uniformity.

Other meats you might like to use instead of or in addition to those listed include firm-fleshed fish such as tuna or swordfish, ground beef, steamed chicken strips, ground turkey and shellfish such as scallops or squid.

Thai spring rolls are tiny and perfect, true finger foods that can be dipped in sauce and eaten in one bite.

At Bangkok Garden, we use 4 1/2-inch (11 cm) square wonton wrappers, which are widely available fresh and frozen. They are just the right size for producing these tasty morsels. Those who need to avoid wheat can purchase the dessert plate-sized 6 1/2-inch (16 cm) rice flour pancakes that are available dried in most Oriental stores. They keep indefinitely. Soak them 5 minutes in warm water to cover, lay on a cloth and roll. You may also be able to find dried rice noodle squares. Chinese spring roll wrappers, widely available in frozen food sections, will produce a thicker spring roll.

Assembling the spring rolls is going to take some time and patience, so make sure you've got a comfortable work surface. It's easiest to work on a clean, damp cloth. Have ready a platter or tray to hold the finished spring rolls and a damp (not wet) cloth to cover them so they don't dry out. Plastic film also works.

TASTE
SLIGHTLY SALTY

You can prepare
bean sprouts
and keep in a
bowl of icy cold
water until you
need them.

Use any size
shrimps—small
salad shrimp
are a good buy
and they are
already shelled
and deveined.

In Thailand the
crabmeat would
be fresh and
raw but in our
experience, pre-
cooked canned
or frozen crab-
meat will do.

4 cups	bean sprouts (10 oz/300 g)	1 L
6	large dried mushrooms	6
3.5 oz	bean thread noodles (2 bundles)	100 g
20	stalks fresh coriander	20
2	green onions	2
1/2 cup	crabmeat	125 mL
1 cup	shrimp (any size)	250 mL
2-3 cups	vegetable oil	500-750 mL
	for deep-frying	
1/2 cup	ground pork	125 mL
1/2 tsp	ground white pepper	2 mL
2 tbsp	fish sauce (or 1 tbsp/15 mL salt)	30 mL
2-4 tsp	fructose (or other sweetener)	10-20 mL
40	square (4 1/2 inch/11 cm)	40
	wonton wrappers	
1	egg yolk, beaten	1

Wash bean sprouts and remove all stringy roots. Drain well.

Soak mushrooms 20-30 minutes in hot water to cover. Rinse well to remove sand and debris, then slice thinly in shreds.

Soak bean thread noodles 10 minutes in warm water to cover. Drain and cut with scissors into 3/4-1 1/2 inch (2-4 cm) lengths.

Chop coriander. If you have the roots, wash them well, pound in a mortar and chop fine. Slice green onions lengthwise 2 or 3 times, then cut into 2-inch (5 cm) lengths. Shred crabmeat. Peel and devein shrimp; chop fine.

Heat a wok on high 2 minutes. Add 1 tbsp (15 mL) oil. Reduce heat to medium and add chopped coriander and roots. Stir briefly a few seconds. Add pork; cook, stirring, 2 minutes. Add shrimp; stir-fry 1 minute. Add bean sprouts, mushrooms, noodles, green onions and crabmeat; cook, stirring, on medium until well mixed and bean sprouts are slightly wilted, about 2 minutes. Remove from heat.

Add pepper, fish sauce and fructose. Mix well and turn into a bowl to stop the cooking process. The filling will keep well up to 24 hours in the refrigerator.

Place each wonton wrapper on work surface so that it is a diamond shape. Place a heaping tablespoonful (15 mL) of filling in the centre of the wrapper and mold the filling into a cylindrical shape with your fingers. Pick up the point of the wrapper closest to you and fold it over the filling so that the wrapper just covers the filling. With the thumb and forefinger of each hand, fold the ends of the wrapper in toward the centre, then roll the whole thing away from you to make a tidy cylindrical roll about the size of your thumb. Brush the edges of the wrapper with a little of the beaten egg to "glue" it together, then place on a tray. Spring rolls can be prepared to this point and kept refrigerated, tightly covered with plastic film or damp cloth, for up to 24 hours. Never fry spring rolls ahead of time and reheat. They will go soggy.

Heat about 2 cups (500 mL) oil in a heavy pot or deep-fryer. Cook 6-10 spring rolls at a time until wonton wrappers are deep golden brown and crispy. (Keep the oil high as you would for french fries; there should be a lot of bubbling and spluttering going on.) Remove and drain on paper towels.

Serve hot with sweet, hot or salty dipping sauces. Crisp, fresh vegetables such as cucumbers and carrots make a nice contrasting accompaniment to these wonderful little snacks. **Makes 40 pieces.**

If you don't have a suitable pot for deep-frying, you can also use a wok—just watch closely to make sure that all sides of the spring rolls get deep-fried.

RELATIVELY
NEUTRAL

THAI SPRING ROLLS: VEGETARIAN

Vegetarians or those who have dietary restrictions can still enjoy wonderful spring rolls. For authenticity, you should use small wrappers, as Thai spring rolls are always tiny, but the wrappers can be made with rice, wheat or bean flour. And as long as you include the key Thai flavouring combination of garlic, coriander, pepper, salt, lime juice and fructose, you can play fast and loose with the other ingredients and still produce something that tastes Thai.

Other ingredients you might like to use instead of or as well as those listed include asparagus, turnip, celery, lotus root or seeds, broccoli, cauliflower, green beans, pumpkin, squash, marrow, snow peas.

Here's how we do it at Bangkok Garden:

6	large dried mushrooms	6
4 cups	bean sprouts (300 g)	1 L
3.5 oz	bean thread noodles (2 bundles)	100 g
3	eggs	3
2 tbsp	fish sauce (or 1 tbsp/15 mL salt) (if desired)	30 mL
1 tsp	ground white pepper	5 mL
2-3 cups	oil for deep-frying	500-750 mL
1 lb	yellow bean curd	500 g
1/2 cup	water chestnuts	125 mL
20	stalks fresh coriander	20
2	green onions	2
4 tbsp	grated carrots	60 mL
1 tbsp	fresh lime juice	15 mL
2 tsp	fructose (or other sweetener)	10 mL
40	square (4 1/2 inch/11 cm) wonton wrappers	40
1	egg yolk	1

Soak mushrooms 30 minutes in hot water to cover. Drain, rinse and slice thinly in lengths. Wash bean sprouts and remove all stringy roots. Soak bean thread noodles 10 minutes in hot water to cover. Cut with scissors into 1 1/2-inch (4 cm) lengths.

Beat 3 eggs well and season with a little fish sauce, if using, and white pepper. Heat a large, heavy, flat-bottomed frying pan for 3 minutes over medium heat. Add 1 tbsp (15 mL) oil; heat 1 minute. Pour in eggs; cook, without stirring, until eggs are set and dry. Remove from pan, allow to cool and cut into very thin strips. (The strips should be very thin, so if pan is small, cook egg in 2 batches.)

Cut yellow bean curd (which is quite hard) into 1 1/2-inch (4 cm) matchsticks. Cut water chestnuts the same way.

Chop coriander. Crush coriander roots and chop fine. Slice green onions lengthwise 2 or 3 times, then cut into 2-inch (5 cm) lengths.

Heat a wok on high 2 minutes. Add 1 tbsp (15 mL) oil. Reduce heat and add chopped coriander and roots. Stir briefly a few seconds. Add bean curd; cook, without stirring, 1-2 minutes or until bean curd turns slightly darker.

Add mushrooms, bean sprouts, bean thread noodles, water chestnuts and green onions; stir-fry on medium heat 2-3 minutes or until bean sprouts are slightly wilted. Remove from heat. Add grated carrots, cooked eggs, lime juice and fructose. Mix well, and put in a bowl to stop the cooking process.

To make up and fry the spring rolls, follow the procedure for Thai Spring Rolls (see page 44). **Makes 40 pieces.**

CHILLI VINEGAR
Prik Nam Som

No Thai table is complete without a bowl or cruet of freshly made chilli vinegar, in case anyone wishes to increase the piquancy and sourness of a prepared dish.

Make this with plain distilled white vinegar and fresh chillies of whatever strength you like, from bird to finger-hot to the milder banana peppers.

Don't keep this sauce around long; discard after 3 days and start again fresh.

| 2 | finger-hot chillies | 2 |
| 4 tbsp | distilled white vinegar | 60 mL |

Wearing rubber gloves, slice chillies into thin rounds. Stir into vinegar and allow to sit for 30 minutes before serving. **Makes about 4 tbsp (60 mL).**

GOLDEN BO LEAVES
Giaw Tod

We call these Golden Bo Leaves because when we fold them a certain way, they resemble the heart-shaped leaves of the Bo tree. Tradition has it that this was the tree the Buddha was meditating under when he attained enlightenment. You could just as easily gather the wrappers up into a sort of grab bag—then they'd be Golden Bundles. Or, fold wontons into any shape you like. Try tying up the bundles with a piece of fresh spaghetti or linguini.

Make sure you use wonton wrappers and not egg roll wrappers to make these crisp little delicacies. The egg roll wrappers will fry up thick and doughy.

25	black peppercorns	25
3	cloves garlic	3
2	fresh coriander roots (or stems if roots unavailable)	2
14 oz	finely ground pork	400 g
1	egg	1
2 tbsp	fish sauce	30 mL
2	green onions, finely chopped	2
60	(approx) wonton wrappers, 3 1/4-inch/8.5 cm square	60
3 cups	vegetable oil for deep-frying	750 mL

Pound peppercorns in a mortar. Crush garlic, then add to mortar and pound with pepper. Chop coriander roots coarsely, add to mortar and pound to a rough paste.

Blend together pork, pounded spices, egg and fish sauce. Mix in green onion.

Have ready a bowl of tepid water to moisten fingers and wonton wrappers. Place each wonton wrapper on work surface so that it is a diamond shape. Brush with water. Place a scant teaspoonful (5 mL) of the filling in the centre and fold wrapper in half away from you—so that the top and bottom points are together. Press edges to seal. Moisten thumbs; grasp right and left ends of the triangle and twist one-quarter turn down (thumbs will push up; forefingers will push down), then press the two pieces down and together with forefingers. You now have a heart shape with the pointed end at the top. (Uncooked filled wrappers can be wrapped in plastic film and refrigerated for up to 24 hours.)

Heat oil in heavy pot or deep-fryer. Deep-fry wontons in oil that is hot but not bubbling 2-3 minutes, or until golden brown. Remove with a slotted spoon and drain on paper towel.

If you don't have a mortar and pestle, grind pepper in a pepper or coffee grinder, or put in a sturdy paper or plastic bag and crush with a blunt implement. Crush garlic cloves and coriander roots, then chop finely. Then chop spice mixture together with knife to blend well.

TASTE

SLIGHTLY SALTY

Serve with sweet and hot dipping sauces, and fresh vegetables for a "green" crunch that will contrast with the "crisp-fried" crunch of the pastries. **Makes 60 pieces.**

STEAMED MUSSELS
Hoy Nung

This classic Thai method of steaming mussels can be used for just about any shellfish and showcases all the favourite lemony-peppery Thai flavours. For piquant mussels, bruise chillies thoroughly and add them to the cooking liquid at the beginning, instead of using them for garnish.

2 lb	fresh mussels	1 kg
1 tbsp	Roasted Chilli Paste (see page 114)	15 mL
3 cups	chicken broth (or water)	750 mL
2	stalks lemon grass, bruised and cut in 1-inch/2.5 cm pieces	2
4	wild lime (makrood) leaves, torn roughly	4
4	slices galanga (kha) root	4
1 tbsp	fish sauce, or to taste	15 mL
	Juice of 1 lime (about 2 tbsp/30 mL), or to taste	
5	stalks fresh coriander	5
6	small hot chillies	6
1	green onion, cut into small pieces	1
	Sriracha sauce	
	Hot and Sour Seafood Dipping Sauce (see page 63)	

Scrub mussels thoroughly, removing beards and all sand. Discard any that do not close.

In saucepan, bring chilli paste and broth to a boil. Add lemon grass, lime leaves, galanga root, fish sauce, lime juice; return to a boil. Add mussels, cover tightly, and cook until the shells open. Discard any that do not open.

Remove each mussel as it opens and arrange on serving platter or mound in a bowl. With a slotted spoon, remove lemon grass, lime leaves and galanga root and sprinkle over mussels. Sprinkle with coriander, hot chillies and green onions. Serve immediately with Sriracha sauce and Hot and Sour Seafood Dipping Sauce. **Serves 4.**

The cooking liquid makes an excellent base for a seafood soup!

TASTE

SALTY
HOT
SOUR

PHOTO:
(in steamer,
clockwise from
top left)
Naughty Little
Peppers
(page 60),
Shrimp Savoy
(page 51),
Curried Mussels
on the Half Shell
(page 58) and
Pork Pearls
(page 52)
shown with
Sriracha Sauce
and Hot and
Sour Seafood
Dipping Sauce
(page 63)

T
A
S
T
E

HOT
SALTY

SPICY SHRIMP PATTIES
Todmun Kung

These frisky little patties resemble mini hamburgers, and in fact can be made with a variety of meats and fish. If all of your guests like their food hot, slice up a few long green chillies in rounds so they resemble the green beans and mix them in. If you want to send a cautionary message to your guests, use fresh red or yellow chillies instead so they can see it's going to be hot. Personally, I prefer the culinary "Russian Roulette" of not knowing whether the little green thing I bite into is going to bite back.

1 lb	shrimp	500 g
4	shallots	4
4	cloves garlic	4
1	stalk lemon grass, bruised and chopped	1
4	fresh coriander roots	4
10	peppercorns (or 1/4 tsp/1 mL cracked black pepper)	10
1	small piece galanga (kha) root (about 2 tsp/10 mL chopped)	1
1	small piece krachai root (about 1 tbsp/15 mL chopped)	1
1/2 tsp	grated wild lime (makrood) peel (lime peel may be substituted)	2 mL
5-10	dried chillies, or to taste	5-10
1 tbsp	shrimp paste (kapi)	15 mL
1 tbsp	fish sauce, or to taste	15 mL
8 oz	green beans, thinly sliced in rounds	250 g
1	egg, beaten	1
2-3 cups	vegetable oil for deep-frying	500-750 mL

Peel and devein shrimp; puree or grind.

In a mortar, pound together shallots, garlic, lemon grass, coriander roots, peppercorns, galanga, krachai, wild lime peel and chillies. Gradually blend in shrimp paste and fish sauce as the ingredients start to break down. When consistency of a fairly smooth paste, mix in shrimp puree, green beans and egg. ➤

Roll into small balls and flatten each ball. Heat oil in heavy pot or deep-fryer; deep-fry patties over medium heat about 4 minutes or until golden.

Serve with a tart, sweet cucumber salad and a hot Sriracha sauce. **Makes 15-20 pieces.**

SHRIMP SAVOY
Makua Tait Savoy

This dish has been designed to yield a generous appetiser for six, but if you're feeling particularly patient, you could stuff large cherry tomatoes instead.

Because the tomatoes are cooked, this dish isn't really a finger food.

6	medium firm red tomatoes	6
25	peppercorns	25
2	fresh coriander roots (or stems if roots are unavailable)	2
3	cloves garlic	3
7 oz	ground pork	200 g
1	egg (or 2 tbsp/30 mL tapioca flour)	1
2 tsp	fish sauce	10 mL
1 tsp	fructose	5 mL
2	shallots, finely chopped (or 3 tbsp/45 mL grated cooking onion)	2
1/2 cup	mixed green peas and corn kernels	125 mL
7 oz	small salad shrimp	200 g

Place tomatoes stem side down; cut off the top third. Scoop out flesh and use for another dish.

In a mortar, pound peppercorns, coriander roots and garlic. Add to ground pork in a bowl. Add egg, fish sauce, fructose and shallots; mix thoroughly. Add peas and corn and shrimp; stir just until mixed.

Divide pork mixture into tomatoes. Steam 15-20 minutes or until cooked through and pork is no longer pink. Lift tomatoes out carefully onto individual serving dishes and serve hot or warm. **Serves 6.**

*PHOTO:
Lemon Shrimp
Soup
(page 67)
shown with bird
chillies, lemon
grass, wild lime
leaves, galanga
root and roasted
chilli paste*

TASTE
SALTY
SWEET

PORK PEARLS
Saku Sai Muu

This tasty tidbit probably has a relative in the steamed dim sum so popular in Southern China.

There have been numerous Chinese influences in Thai cuisine. The present-day Thai people are descended from a group that migrated from Southern China in about AD 800—and in fact there is still an ethnic Thai population in Southern China, the descendants of those who remained behind.

During the Ming Dynasty (1368-1644), a small but culturally influential group of Chinese potters settled in Thailand to establish porcelain factories. Another major migration occurred in the mid-19th century when a Chinese merchant class settled in Bangkok, their settlement forming a large Chinatown, which is still an important landmark in central Bangkok. Was it a Chinese chef who decided to make a dim sum with Thai ingredients? More likely it was an inventive Thai chef, taken with the idea of tiny, tasty steamed dumplings, who put this charming spin on the concept.

Whatever the origin, these shimmering pearly balls of chewy tapioca filled with a sweet-salty pork mixture make wonderful appetizers. Serve warm with tiny hot chillies and fresh coriander leaves.

At Bangkok Garden, we have also made these with chicken, fish or bean curd instead of pork in order to accommodate guests' dietary requirements.

Filling

4 tbsp	light vegetable oil	60 mL
10	cloves garlic, coarsely chopped	10
5	shallots, sliced	5
15	stalks fresh coriander	15
3/4 lb	lean ground pork	350 g
4 tbsp	chopped salted turnip	60 mL
4 tbsp	crushed unroasted peanuts (see page 22)	60 mL
1 tsp	ground black pepper	5 mL
2 tbsp	fish sauce	30 mL
4 tbsp	palm sugar (or other sweetener)	60 mL

Dough

3 cups	small pearl tapioca	750 mL
1 1/2 cups	boiling water	375 mL

Filling: Heat oil in a wok over medium heat and fry garlic until light brown. Remove with a slotted spoon; drain on paper towel. Fry shallots in same way and set aside for garnish. Remove leaves from coriander stalks and set aside for garnish. Finely chop stems for use in meat mixture.

In the same wok, stir-fry the pork until light brown. Stir in turnips, peanuts, pepper, fish sauce and palm sugar. Reduce heat and cook 10 minutes or until no longer runny. Remove from heat. When cool, add half the fried garlic and all the chopped coriander stems and mix well.

Dough: In saucepan, soak tapioca for 3 minutes in enough water to cover. Drain well. Stir in 1 1/2 cups (375 mL) boiling water and cook 5 minutes over low heat, stirring occasionally, until water is completely absorbed and mixture is very stiff. Let cool to lukewarm.

Have ready a bowl of water to moisten your hands. Drop a heaping teaspoonful (5 mL) of lukewarm dough onto a smooth oiled surface; flatten into a circle with the heel of your hand. Drop a spoonful of the pork mixture onto the centre and pinch the edges of the dough together to form a ball.

Place balls, pinched side down, in oiled steamer, making sure they don't touch each other. Cover and steam 10-12 minutes or until shiny and translucent.

Serve on lettuce leaves. Sprinkle with remaining fried garlic, reserved fried shallot and coriander leaves. Tiny hot bird chillies make an excellent accompaniment to this unusual and attractive appetizer. **Makes about 40 pieces. Most people will eat between 1 and 3 pieces.**

Meat will be easier to slice thinly if placed in freezer for 1 to 2 hours.

SWEET AND SALTY AIR-DRIED BEEF
Nua Sawaan

This is a favourite cocktail-hour snack, and one greatly favoured by card players. Teamed with sticky rice and a tangy Northern-Style Papaya Salad (Som Tam) it makes a great lunch, light dinner or picnic. This dish is not recommended for those with tender teeth. If you require a more tender dish, use top butt or other more tender cuts of beef. Thais prefer this dish chewy! Choose meat that is marbled with fat.

1 lb	flank steak	500 g
4 tbsp	fructose	60 mL
4 tbsp	fish sauce	60 mL
2 tsp	vegetable oil	10 mL
2 tbsp	coriander seeds	30 mL
2-3 cups	vegetable oil	500-750 mL
	for deep-frying	

Slice beef very thinly across the grain and place in a large bowl. Combine fructose, fish sauce and 2 tsp (10 mL) oil; toss with the beef.

Test for desired sweetness and saltiness by grilling or deep-frying a piece of beef. It should taste just a little less sweet than you want the final product to taste. Final cooking will increase the sweetness. Adjust seasonings if necessary.

Pound coriander seeds lightly until coarse. Pound into the beef with a mallet or a heavy bottle.

Spread the slices on an oven rack and leave in a warm, airy place until dry (12-24 hours). Or put rack in turned off oven after removing dinner; the meat will be dried in the retained heat by morning. Store air-dried beef in airtight container in a refrigerator or cool place for up to 2 weeks.

Heat oil in heavy pot or deep-fryer; deep-fry air-dried beef 2 minutes until crisp. Drain on paper towel. Serve at room temperature with sticky rice, fresh vegetables and a bowl of roasted peanuts. **Serves 8.**

TASTE

SWEET
SALTY

GALLOPING HORSES
Ma Ho

This unusual hors d'oeuvre combining meat and fruit can be very exciting visually if you pile the meat mixture onto several different types of fruit. To accommodate guests' dietary requirements, we have substituted chicken or bean curd for the pork with excellent results.

6	cloves garlic	6
4	shallots	4
6	fresh coriander roots	6
2 tbsp	vegetable oil	30 mL
1 lb	lean ground pork	500 g
4 tbsp	coarsely crushed unroasted peanuts (see page 22)	60 mL
2 tbsp	fish sauce	30 mL
4 tbsp	chopped salted turnip	60 mL
1/4 tsp	finely ground white (or black) pepper	1 mL
1/2 tsp	palm sugar (or other sweetener)	2 mL
	Fresh pineapple pieces	
	Canned rambutans (unsweetened)	
	Orange slices	
2	chillies, slivered	2
	Mint or coriander sprigs for garnish	

In a mortar, crush garlic, shallots and coriander roots. Heat oil in a wok over low heat. Add garlic mixture and stir-fry until golden. Add pork, peanuts, fish sauce, turnip, pepper and palm sugar; stir-fry until dark brown and dry. Keep the heat at low about 10 minutes; do not try to rush this part of the cooking. Let cool.

Arrange pineapple, drained rambutans and oranges on a serving platter. Pile the cooled pork mixture onto the fruit pieces. Garnish with chilli slivers or fiery bird chillies and sprigs of mint or coriander leaves. Chill until ready to serve. **Makes about 50 pieces. Most people will eat between 2 and 5 pieces.**

TASTE

SALTY
SWEET

STEAMED CRAB CAKE
Puu Ja

This hearty appetiser has its origins on the Gulf of Siam and has almost as many subtle variations as there are towns and villages along the coast of the bountiful Gulf.

I have chosen this simple version, assuming you'll be using frozen or canned crab—or possibly even crab-flavoured pollack.

In Thailand, where live crabs are now available even very far inland, Puu Ja is made with fresh crab, and the preferred way to steam and serve it is in its own shell.

You may be able to obtain crab shells from your local fish market. Otherwise, use large scallop shells, ramekins or even a single large mold.

2 cups	crabmeat (11 oz/320 g)	500 mL
2	fresh coriander roots	2
2 tsp	finely chopped coriander leaves	10 mL
1 1/2 cups	fresh bread crumbs	375 mL
1/2 tsp	finely ground pepper	2 mL
1 tsp	salt	5 mL
1	cooking onion, finely chopped (about 1 cup/250 mL)	1
3	green onions, chopped	3
1	egg, lightly beaten	1
1	egg yolk	1
	Sriracha sauce	

Shred crabmeat. Pound coriander roots, then chop fine. Combine crab, coriander roots and leaves, bread crumbs, pepper, salt, onion, green onions and egg. Mix together well.

Pour into 4 lightly oiled bowls. Brush tops with beaten egg yolk. Steam 30 minutes. Cooking time will depend on size and shape of molds: cook small molds 20 minutes; one large mold 45 minutes.

Cool and serve warm or lukewarm on a bed of lettuce with Sriracha sauce on the side. **Serves 4.**

TASTE
SWEET
SALTY

GOLDEN DAWN CHICKEN WINGS
Peek Gai Yatsai

These crispy golden chicken wings make a very hearty appetiser: one per person may be quite enough, depending on how many other dishes you're serving.

It's the particular flavour of the coriander root that gives the meat filling its unique flavour.

12	chicken wings	12
25	black peppercorns	25
2	fresh coriander roots (substitute stems if roots are unavailable)	2
3	large cloves garlic	3
14 oz	ground pork	400 g
2 tbsp	fish sauce	30 mL
1	egg, lightly beaten	1
2	green onions, finely chopped	2
12	short bamboo skewers	12
2-3 cups	light vegetable oil for deep-frying	500-750 mL

Remove bone from largest section of each chicken wing keeping the flesh of the wing intact. (Save the bones for soup stock.)

In a mortar, pound together peppercorns, coriander roots and garlic. Blend into ground pork in a bowl. Add fish sauce, egg and green onions; mix thoroughly. Stuff into the cavity left by the bone. Close with a bamboo skewer.

Heat oil in a heavy pot, wok or deep-fryer. Fry wings, 3-4 at a time, until skin is crispy and a deep golden brown. Drain.

Serve hot with sweet and hot dipping sauces, found on pages 62-63. Makes 12 pieces.

TASTE
SLIGHTLY
SALTY

CURRIED MUSSELS ON THE HALF SHELL
Hormok Hoy

Hormok is one of those Thai curiosities that defies description. It's a curry, but it's solid, steamed in banana leaves until the pungent coconut-curry gravy is set like a custard. Nestled in this aromatic curry custard you could find almost any sea creature.

The traditional Thai container for hormok is a banana leaf formed into a cup shape: large for a main course, tiny for an appetiser. Our version uses the mussel's own shell as the container. This appetiser can be prepared ahead of time and frozen before steaming—a rare luxury as most Thai dishes must be prepared only moments before serving.

2 lb	fresh mussels	1 kg
1 tbsp	light vegetable oil	15 mL
2 tbsp	Red Curry Paste (see page 104)	30 mL
	(or 2 tbsp/30 mL Kua Curry Paste	
	(see page 108) and 2 tbsp/30 mL	
	shrimp paste (kapi))	
1	duck egg (or hen egg), beaten	1
3/4 cup	coconut cream	200 mL
2 tsp	rice flour	10 mL
1 tsp	fish sauce	5 mL
1 tsp	ground white pepper	5 mL
5	stalks fresh Thai basil	5
2	finger-hot chillies, finely shredded	2
2	wild lime (makrood) leaves,	2
	finely shredded	
	Coriander or fresh fennel leaves, if desired	

Scrub mussels thoroughly, removing beards and all sand. Discard any that do not close. Steam just until shells open, discarding any that do not open. Remove mussels from the shell. Reserve half the shells.

Heat oil in a pan and sauté Red Curry Paste over medium heat until fragrant, about 2 minutes. Combine in a bowl with egg, coconut cream, rice flour, fish sauce and pepper.

Remove basil leaves from stalks and blanch briefly in boiling water. Line each mussel shell with one or two leaves. Put a mussel in each shell; cover with coconut-curry mixture. Sprinkle with chillies and wild lime (makrood) leaves. Steam 5 minutes or

TASTE

HOT

until coconut mixture sets. Garnish with fresh coriander or fennel. Makes 20-30 pieces. Most people will eat 1-3 pieces.

CRISPY SHRIMP BALLS
Kung Grob

This crispy appetiser has been on our menu since Bangkok Garden opened in 1982. It takes some patience to make it at home as it must be deep-fried very gently.

The good news is that you can use a meat grinder or food processor to prepare the shrimp.

1 lb	raw shrimp	500 g
1	egg white	1
1 tsp	salt	5 mL
1/2 tsp	ground pepper	2 mL
1 tbsp	cornstarch (or tapioca flour)	15 mL
8-10	slices white bread	8-10
3 cups	light vegetable oil for deep-frying	750 mL

In a mortar, grinder or food processor, pound shrimp until sticky. Mince very fine, then mix in egg white, salt, pepper and cornstarch. Form into quite sticky balls about the size of large marbles.

Remove crusts from bread. Cut bread into miniature cubes about the size of peas. Roll each ball in bread cubes until coated.

Heat oil in a wok over medium heat until hot but not smoking. (Wok should be no more than 1/3 full of hot oil.)

Fry balls gently until bread is toasted brown, 3-5 minutes. Drain on paper towel and serve with dipping sauces, found on pages 62-63. Makes about 50 pieces.

The deep-frying oil should not be smoking: if oil is too hot, the bread will over-cook while the shrimp stays raw. Patience is the key to this one.

T
A
S
T
E
NEARLY
NEUTRAL

NAUGHTY LITTLE PEPPERS
Prik Youack Yatsai

This is one of the very few Thai dishes that's suited to the microwave. Cook at high approximately 5 minutes over a reservoir of boiling water.

Wear rubber gloves when preparing hot peppers—they will sting your hands and eyes.

T
A
S
T
E
HOT

We developed this dish in response to customer demand for hotter and hotter foods. It made its first appearance at one of our wildly popular Chilli Pepper Festivals.

Make this dish even naughtier by using finger-hot or jalapeño peppers if your guests are up to it! To turn this into a milder dish, omit the hot chillies in the pork mixture, or substitute chopped green beans.

At Bangkok Garden, the chefs lament that customers often eat the meat filling and leave the banana pepper. At home, it's OK to remind your guests that banana peppers are an excellent source of Vitamin C!

20	banana peppers	20
7 oz	raw shrimp	200 g
7 oz	ground pork	200 g
25	black peppercorns (1/2 tsp/2 mL cracked black pepper)	25
2	fresh coriander roots	2
3	cloves garlic	3
4	shallots (or 1 cooking onion), finely chopped	4
1/2 tsp	ground nutmeg	2 mL
1	green onion, finely chopped	1
4	finger-hot chillies, or to taste, finely chopped	4
1 tbsp	fish sauce	15 mL
2 tbsp	chopped fresh coriander leaves	30 mL
1	egg, beaten (or 1 tbsp/15 mL tapioca flour)	1
	Lettuce and fresh vegetables such as carrot, cucumber rounds, snow peas, cauliflower or broccoli florets for garnish	

Wash banana peppers and slit lengthwise. Remove seeds if desired. Set aside.

Peel, devein and finely mince shrimp. Combine in a bowl with the ground pork.

In a mortar, pound together peppercorns, coriander roots, garlic and shallots to a moist paste. Add to meat, together with nutmeg, green onion, chillies, fish sauce, coriander leaves and egg. Knead thoroughly until well mixed.

Form mixture into tube shapes and press into banana peppers, filling all interior spaces. Steam peppers, slit side up, for 10 minutes or until pork is no longer pink and peppers are soft.

Arrange peppers on serving plates. Garnish with lettuce and vegetables and serve with hot dipping sauce and sticky rice. Makes 20 pieces. We serve 3 on a plate as an appetiser but if you are serving other appetisers you may find 1 or 2 per person is plenty.

SPICY CUCUMBER SALAD
Aatjaat

This tiny, tangy salad is most popularly served as an accompaniment to Satay, Spicy Shrimp Patties and Naughty Little Peppers. Serve it whenever you need something sweet, sour, hot or crunchy. It is clearly a Thai rendition of the Indian "ajar" or pickle. For extra colour, add thinly sliced carrots.

1	cucumber, about 8 inches/20 cm	1
2	red chillies	2
3	shallots	3
2 tbsp	vinegar	30 mL
2 tsp	fructose (or other sweetener)	10 mL
1 tsp	fish sauce	5 mL

Quarter unpeeled cucumber lengthwise and slice thinly crosswise. Slice chillies thinly in rounds. Slice shallots thinly. Place vegetables in bowl.

Combine vinegar, fructose and fish sauce, stirring until fructose dissolves. Pour over cucumber mixture; refrigerate about 30 minutes before serving. Makes 1 cup (250 mL).

Variation: Some people like to heat the dressing to the boil before pouring it over the vegetables. This just wilts the veggies slightly and allows the dressing to penetrate. Cool to room temperature before serving.

To prepare this side dish ahead of time, cover and refrigerate vegetables and dressing separately. Pour dressing over the vegetables just before serving.

TASTE
SWEET
SOUR
HOT

TASTE

SWEET

SWEET DIPPING SAUCE
Nam Prik Waan

For those who don't like chillies and ginger, you can tint the sauce with 1/2 tsp (2 mL) sweet paprika which will give it a yellow tone.

1 cup	fructose	250 mL
1/2 cup	vinegar	125 mL
1 tbsp	salt	15 mL
1-3 tsp	thinly shredded fresh ginger, carrot and/or red chillies	5-15 mL

Combine fructose, vinegar and salt in a small saucepan, bring to a boil, reduce heat and simmer 10 minutes. Remove from heat, stir in shredded ginger, carrot and/or chillies. Let cool. Sauce can be refrigerated up to 2 days, or many weeks if no vegetables are added. Serve in small individual bowls.

Makes 3/4 cup, (175 mL), enough to accompany 40 Thai spring rolls.

TASTE

HOT
SALTY

HOT AND SALTY SAUCE
Prik Nam Pla

Serve as an accompaniment to any dish you may wish to make saltier or hotter. Remember the heat in the sauce depends on the kind of chillies you use.

2	fresh chillies	2
2 tbsp	fish sauce	30 mL
	Juice of 1 lime, or to taste	

Bruise chillies slightly with the flat of a knife; slice or chop fine and add to fish sauce. Let stand 30 minutes to allow chilli flavour to develop. Add lime juice to taste. **Makes about 1/4 cup (60 mL).**

HOT AND SOUR SEAFOOD DIPPING SAUCE
Nam Chim Pla

This sauce is good with all types of seafood. Bruise the chillies with the flat of a knife before chopping to release the oil of capsaicin, which is the chief "biting" agent in chillies. The sauce is best when eaten within 8 hours of making.

2	stalks fresh coriander	2
4	fresh chillies, bruised and finely chopped	4
2	cloves garlic, bruised and finely chopped	2
2	shallots, thinly sliced	2
1 tsp	fructose	5 mL
	Juice of 2 limes	
2 tbsp	fish sauce	30 mL

Remove coriander leaves from stalks and chop stalks finely. In bowl, combine coriander stalks, chillies, garlic, shallots, fructose, lime juice and fish sauce, stirring to dissolve fructose. Let stand for at least 30 minutes to allow flavours to develop. Serve in small dishes. Float coriander leaves on top. **Makes about 1/2 cup (125 mL).**

SWEET PLUM SAUCE
Nam Chim Waan

The flavour of this sauce is largely up to personal taste. Thais feel it should be more sweet than sour, but like to add the vinegar for the bite. You can also add a few shreds of fresh grated ginger.

1 cup	Chinese plums in vinegar	250 mL
4 tbsp	honey, or to taste	60 mL
1/2 cup	water	125 mL
1 tsp	salt, or to taste	5 mL

In saucepan, combine plums, honey, water and salt. Bring to a boil, cover and simmer gently 10 minutes. Sieve to remove plum pits. **Makes about 1 1/2 cups (375 mL).**

If plums in vinegar are unavailable, use dried plums soaked in hot water (about 1 cup/250 mL) and 3-4 tablespoons/45-60 mL vinegar, or to taste, until soft.

Fresh Canadian plums in season also work with this sauce, but not dried prunes. Peel, pit and puree fresh plums and add 3-4 tablespoons/45-60 mL vinegar, to taste.

CHAPTER 5
SOUPS

* * * * * *

Most Thai meals featuring two or more dishes are accompanied by a clear soup, served in tiny bowls throughout the meal from a charcoal-fired steamboat, which is often placed on a side stand to protect diners from the heat it radiates.

These soups, based on lightly flavoured meat or fish broths, contain relatively small amounts of vegetables, meat or fish. Diners consume several bowls throughout the main course, in much the same way the Chinese drink clear green tea. Clear soups, called Gaeng Juut, are a way of clearing the palate between bites of rich or spicy main dishes.

Simple stock made with chicken or pork bones (or both) is the basis for Gaeng Juut. They take their subtle flavours from the ingredients featured—shreds of meat, sliced vegetables, tiny garlicky meatballs.

Most Thai cooks make their soup stocks daily; you and I may find it more practical to make larger quantities and freeze some for later use.

Tom Yum soups, the hot, sour and lemony soups Thailand is famous for, are clear broths strongly flavoured with galanga root, lemon grass and wild lime leaves and made incendiary with tiny hot bird chillies. In Thailand these are also served in tiny bowls as an accompaniment to the main courses.

Gai Tom Kha, the sinfully silky Coconut Chicken soup, is really a Tom Yum made with coconut milk and coconut cream. It is so rich that some consider it a curry, spooning it over steamed rice and eating it like a main course.

Several other soups are to be found in other chapters. Gaeng Som can be served either soup-style or as a main course; I put it in the curry chapter because it is made with curry paste.

Some rice and noodle soups such as Midnight Soup (see page 168) are considered a meal in a bowl and would not be served as part of a multi-course lunch or dinner, so I put them in Chapter 10 with the other rice and noodle dishes.

At Bangkok Garden—and indeed in my own home—I've found that people prefer to eat the way they're used to eating, and so we tend to serve the soups as a separate course. You should serve your soups in whatever way makes you and your guests most comfortable.

CHICKEN STOCK

If you don't have bones, buy backs and necks. This will definitely give you a fattier broth. If necessary, refrigerate the stock and lift off the fat after it hardens.

2 lb	chicken bones	1 kg
24 cups	water	6 L

Remove skin and fat from bones. Put in a large pot or soup kettle, add water and bring to boil. Reduce heat to medium and cook at a low boil 30 minutes. Skim off any foam. Strain and if necessary skim off any fat. **Makes about 16 cups (4 L).**

PORK STOCK

Use only fresh—not smoked—bones. Ask your butcher for trimmed neck bones, which seem to deliver the best flavour.

2 lb	fresh pork bones	1 kg
24 cups	water	6 L

Put bones in a large pot, add water and bring to boil. Boil hard, skimming off any foam, for 5-10 minutes or until soup stops foaming. Reduce heat slightly and continue boiling 30 minutes. Discard bones; strain if necessary. **Makes about 16 cups (4 L).**

BEEF STOCK

Knuckle bones, shins, ribs or neck bones without too much meat clinging to them are best.

2 lb	fresh beef bones, well trimmed	1 kg
24 cups	water	6 L

Put bones in a large pot, add water and bring to the boil. Boil hard, skimming off any foam, for 5-10 minutes or until soup stops foaming. Reduce heat slightly and continue boiling 30 minutes. Discard bones; strain if necessary. **Makes about 16 cups (4 L).**

If beef and pork bones are hard to get, chicken stock will do fine for most Thai soups. Even when the meat in the soup is pork balls or beef shreds, the chicken stock is an excellent base on which to build.

SHRIMP SHELL STOCK

This is a delightful Thai way to add extra fresh flavour to soups containing fish, shellfish or shrimps. We use this method for Tom Yum Kung and Gaeng Som Kung where the extra "shrimpiness" can best be appreciated.

8 cups	chicken stock (or water)	2 L
	Shells from 2 lb/1 kg raw shrimp	
	(heads too, if they are on)	

In large pot, bring chicken stock to a full rolling boil. Add shells and boil hard 8 minutes. Strain. **Makes about 7 cups (1.75 L).**

CRISPY FRIED GARLIC AND CRISPY FRIED GARLIC IN OIL

Use Crispy Fried Garlic in Oil to dress soups and noodle dishes. The garlicky oil adds an extra richness to clear soups and plain vegetables. The dry garlic can be sprinkled on almost anything as a finishing touch and can make a major difference in the impact the dish makes on your taste buds.

8	heads garlic (about	8
	1 cup/250 mL chopped)	
3 cups	light vegetable oil	750 mL

Shallots or small red onions (bom daeng) can be sliced and deep-fried the same way but should be used the same day they are prepared as they tend to go soggy over time.

Peel garlic, then smash each clove with the flat of a knife or other blunt implement. Chop roughly with a sharp knife. You should have small chunks about the size of a peppercorn—the final product should be big enough to deliver a toasty crunch.

Heat oil in a wok until it just begins to smoke. When you add the garlic it will hiss and splutter and foam up quite violently, so be prepared. I pile the garlic on a slotted spoon so my hand is well back from the spluttering.

As the foam dies down, stir with a slotted spoon, scraping the bottom continually as the garlic does have a tendency to stick. Watch the garlic carefully. As soon as it turns toasty golden, remove from the pan with the slotted spoon to a paper towel and allow to dry for half an hour.

Pour the oil into a storage jar and when it has cooled, add half the crispy fried garlic to it.

Put the other half into a clean dry storage jar and cover both tightly. Both will keep at room temperature for many weeks.

LEMON SHRIMP SOUP
Tom Yum Kung

One of the greatest delights of a Thai meal is a steamboat brimming with Tom Yum Kung, the tart and tangy shrimp soup that is almost a national institution. Thais like this soup blisteringly hot. It is possible to leave out most or all of the chillies and chilli paste and still produce a delightful soup for guests who just can't take the heat.

1 tbsp	Roasted Chilli Paste (see page 114)	15 mL
2 1/2 cups	chicken stock (or shrimp shell stock) (see pages 65-66)	625 mL
1	stalk fresh lemon grass, bruised and thinly sliced (or 4 tbsp/60 mL dried)	1
2	wild lime (makrood) leaves, torn (not cut) in small pieces	2
8	thin slices galanga (kha) root	8
1 tsp	fish sauce, or to taste	5 mL
8	straw mushrooms, cut in half	8
4 oz	raw shrimp (about 12 pieces)	120 g
	Juice of 1 lime (about 2 tbsp/30 mL), or to taste	
	Leaves from 2 stalks fresh coriander	
6	small hot chillies	6
1	green onion, coarsely chopped	1

Combine chilli paste and stock in a saucepan and bring to the boil. Add lemon grass, wild lime leaves, galanga root, fish sauce, straw mushrooms; return to the boil. Add shrimp; cook about 1 minute until liquid returns to the boil and shrimp are pink. Remove from heat. Add lime juice.

Taste for seasonings. To increase the saltiness, add more fish sauce. Increase the sour sensation with the addition of lime juice. To make the soup more piquant, crush or gently pound the small hot chillies before adding them to the soup.

To finish off the soup, garnish with coriander leaves, hot chillies and green onions. Serve immediately. **Serves 4.**

It's important to tear wild lime leaves when you're using large pieces. When the leaves are cut with a knife, the cells will rush to seal themselves up again, trapping the flavour oils inside. Tearing creates a more ragged cut along more surfaces, releasing more oils.

TASTE
HOT
SOUR

CRISPY FISH SOUP WITH GREEN MANGO
Tom Yum Pla Grob

Don't let this soup sit around once you've added the fish and toasted chillies. Part of its charm is the surprise of finding crispy fish in a bowl of soup! You may even want to carry the fish to the table on a small tray and add it to the soup after everyone has settled down.

1 lb	rainbow (or brook) trout fillets	500 g
2-3 cups	vegetable oil for deep-frying	500-750 mL
6 cups	chicken stock (or shrimp shell stock) (see pages 65-66)	1.5 L
4	stalks lemon grass, bruised and cut in 1-inch/2.5 cm lengths	4
2-4	shallots, sliced	2-4
4-8	wild lime (makrood) leaves	4-8
4 tbsp	green mango, sliced in matchstick shape or shredded Thai style, as for green papaya (see page 87)	60 mL
4 tbsp	tamarind puree	60 mL
1/2 cup	fish sauce	125 mL
2 tbsp	chopped green onion	30 mL
2 tbsp	chopped fresh coriander	30 mL
6-10	dry-roasted dried chillies (see page 29)	6-10

Cut fish into bite-sized lengths; pat dry. Heat oil in heavy pot or deep-fryer. Deep-fry fish until brown and crispy. Drain on a paper towel. In saucepan, bring chicken stock to boil. Add lemon grass, shallots, lime leaves, green mango, tamarind puree and fish sauce. Simmer for about 3 minutes. Taste and adjust seasonings.

Pour into bowls, add fish, green onion, coriander and chillies and serve immediately. **Serves 4.**

TASTE

HOT
SOUR

TIGER LILY SOUP
Gaeng Juut Dock Maay Cheen

In the North of Thailand, in the fields around Chiang Mai, farmers grow thousands of tiger lilies, which are never allowed to flower. The buds are harvested just as they are about to open, and for two or three weeks the vegetable markets are filled with baskets of the finger-length green buds. Stir-fried with fish sauce and garlic, the tender young buds make a delicious vegetable dish not unlike fresh asparagus. What can't be eaten fresh is sun-dried for use year-round in this light and unusual soup.

2 oz	bean thread noodles (1 bundle)	50 g
3.5 oz	dried tiger lily buds	100 g
2	green onions	2
5 cups	chicken stock (see page 65)	1.25 L
3.5 oz	lean pork, finely chopped	100 g
2 tsp	fish sauce, or to taste	10 mL
2	stalks fresh coriander	2
	Freshly ground white pepper to taste	

Cover noodles with warm water and soak for 10 minutes until soft; drain. Cover dried tiger lily buds with hot water and soak 10 minutes or until soft. Drain, and tie each bud in a knot—otherwise the petals will spread out, giving the soup an untidy appearance. Chop tops of green onions and reserve for garnish. Quarter white part of green onions lengthwise and cut in 1 1/2-inch (4 cm) lengths.

In saucepan, bring stock to a boil. Add pork, tiger lily buds and green onion lengths; boil 5 minutes. Reduce heat, add noodles and simmer 2-3 minutes. Season with fish sauce.

Pour into a serving bowl and sprinkle with onion tops, fresh coriander and a grating of pepper. **Serves 4.**

Bean thread noodles are commonly sold in large packages containing 10-12 individual bundles; one of these is enough for soup for 4.

TASTE
SLIGHTLY
SALTY

COCONUT CHICKEN SOUP
Gai Tom Kha

This hearty, zesty dish sits on the border between soup and main course. Served with steamed rice and a bowl of crisp raw vegetables, it makes a great lunch or light supper. In a Thai household the chicken would be chopped into bite-sized chunks with a meat cleaver. If the bones are splintered, so much the better; they add good flavour to the dish. At Bangkok Garden, in deference to Western tastes, we use boneless chicken breast. Although it is less elegant, the soup is tastier with the bones left in.

1	chicken (approx 2 lb/1 kg or 1 1/4 to 1 1/2 lb/625-750 g) boneless chicken)	1
1	galanga (kha) root piece (6 inches/15 cm)	1
4 cups	coconut milk	1 L
2	stalks lemon grass, bruised and cut in 1-inch/ 2.5 cm lengths	2
2 cups	coconut cream	500 mL
4	wild lime (makrood) leaves, roughly torn in quarters	4
2 tbsp	lime juice	30 mL
1 tbsp	fish sauce	15 mL
8	small hot chillies, or to taste	8
1	green onion, chopped	1
	Leaves from 2 stalks fresh coriander	

Wash and dry the chicken (if using boneless, skip this step) and cut into bite-sized pieces. Wash galanga root and cut into thin rounds.

In saucepan, bring coconut milk to the boil. Add chicken, lemon grass and galanga root and return to the boil. Lower heat to medium and cook 20 minutes. To prepare ahead, cool, then cover and refrigerate for up to 24 hours.

Bring soup back to the boil, reduce heat. Add coconut cream, wild lime leaves, lime juice, fish sauce and chillies (bruised if you want a hotter soup). Heat through slowly just to boiling point. Do not allow to boil vigorously as this will cause oil to separate from coconut cream.

TASTE

SWEET
HOT
(IF DESIRED)

Taste for seasoning. To increase sourness, add lime juice. To make soup saltier, add fish sauce. Serve immediately, garnished with green onion and coriander leaves. **Serves 4-6.**

BABY CORN SOUP
Gaeng Juut Khaopote On

Miniature ears of corn wrapped in a blanket of lightly spiced pork make this a lovely-to-look-at soup. It's nice to serve this one in individual glass bowls.

5	stalks fresh coriander	5
10 oz	lean ground pork	300 g
1 tsp	ground pepper	5 mL
1 tsp	fish sauce	5 mL
2	cloves garlic, minced	2
12	drained whole baby corn ears	12
5 cups	chicken stock (see page 65)	1.25 L
	Freshly ground white pepper	

Remove leaves from coriander stalks and set aside. Chop stalks. In bowl, combine coriander stalks, pork, pepper, fish sauce and garlic. Mix well.

Flatten a teaspoonful (5 mL) of the pork mixture into a rough triangle. Wrap around a corn ear, making sure only the centre of the corn is covered. Repeat with remaining corn.

In saucepan, bring stock to the boil. Add corn, and return to the boil. Reduce heat and gently simmer 10 minutes. Serve in individual glass bowls, garnished with coriander leaves and white pepper. **Serves 4.**

TASTE
SLIGHTLY
SALTY

CHILLI-LIME OYSTER SOUP
Tom Yum Hoy Nang Lom

For a hot soup, bruise or smash chillies to release added oil of capsaicin. For a milder soup, use milder chillies and add them to the soup whole.

This rich and lemony soup can be as hot or mild as you like. Make it with any kind of fresh shellfish, or even mix types together. Try this dish with scallops or the more economical mussels. Serve a bowl of steamed rice on the side (especially if you make the soup extra piquant) and alternate bites of neutral rice with spoons of tangy oysters.

2 lb	fresh oysters	1 kg
8	slices (fresh or dried) galanga (kha) root	8
4	stalks fresh coriander	4
1-2 tsp	Roasted Chilli Paste (see page 114)	5-10 mL
5 cups	chicken (or shrimp shell) stock (see pages 65-66)	1.25 L
2	stalks lemon grass, bruised well and thinly sliced	2
4	wild lime (makrood) leaves, torn roughly	4
1 tbsp	fish sauce	15 mL
8-12	straw mushrooms, halved (1 7 1/2-oz/213 mL can)	8-12
6	small hot chillies, or to taste	6
	Juice of 1 lime, or to taste	
1	green onion, finely chopped	1

Wash oysters thoroughly, scrubbing well to remove all sand. Discard any that do not close.

Wash fresh galanga root and slice thinly in rounds, or soak dried galanga slices at least 2 hours in water to cover. If using dried galanga root, add the soaking water to the soup as well.

Tear coriander leaves off the stalks and leave whole. Chop stalks into 3/4-inch (2 cm) lengths. Reserve for garnish.

Combine chilli paste and stock in a saucepan and bring to the boil. Add lemon grass, wild lime leaves and galanga root, bring to the boil and boil 5 minutes. Add oysters and cook until shells open. Remove oysters with a slotted spoon; discard any that don't open. Remove the oysters from their shells and put them into a warmed soup tureen, adding a few shells for effect. Keep warm.

TASTE
HOT
SOUR

To broth, add fish sauce, straw mushrooms and chillies; simmer 5 minutes. Remove from heat and stir in lime juice. Taste for seasonings. To increase saltiness, add more fish sauce. Increase the sour sensation by adding lime juice. To make the soup more piquant, crush or pound the fresh chillies or stir in a little more chilli paste.

Pour simmering broth over the oysters in tureen. Sprinkle with green onion and fresh coriander. Serve immediately. Serves 6.

STUFFED CUCUMBER SOUP
Gaeng Juut Taengkwa Yatsai

Small pickling cucumbers stuffed with a lightly spiced pork mixture are the features of this refreshing soup. Make it in August through October when smaller cucumbers are available. At other times, use salad-sized cucumbers cut in 6 pieces. As long as you simmer the soup gently, the filling won't fall out!

12	pickling cucumbers (or 2 large salad-size cucumbers)	12
3	stalks fresh coriander	3
7 oz	lean ground pork	200 g
2	cloves garlic, minced	2
1 tsp	pepper	5 mL
1 tsp	fish sauce	5 mL
5 cups	pork stock (see page 65)	1.25 L
	Freshly ground white pepper	

Peel cucumbers and cut the tip off one end. With a small sharp knife, scoop out the soft centre. Remove leaves from coriander stalks and reserve for garnishing; chop stalks coarsely. In bowl, combine pork, garlic, pepper, fish sauce and coriander stalks. Mix well and stuff into cucumbers.

In saucepan, bring stock to the boil. Add stuffed cucumbers and boil gently 10-15 minutes or until cucumbers are a clear, glassy pale green. Place in a serving bowl and garnish with coriander leaves and a grating of white pepper. **Serves 4.**

TASTE

SLIGHTLY
SALTY

WATERCRESS SOUP WITH PORK BALLS
Gaeng Juut Pak Bung

When cooked, watercress is quite bitter, which is an important consideration when you're searching for a dish to round off your taste combinations (sweet, sour, hot, salty, bitter). This soup also works well with other leafy greens such as spinach, Swiss chard, beet or turnip greens.

10	peppercorns	10
1	clove garlic	1
1	fresh coriander root (optional)	1
2 tsp	fish sauce	10 mL
3.5 oz	lean pork, ground extra fine	100 g
1 1/2 cups	watercress (1 large bunch)	375 mL
5 cups	chicken stock (see page 65)	1.25 L
2	green onions, finely chopped	2

In a mortar, pound together peppercorns, garlic, and fresh coriander root if desired, to a fine paste. Add fish sauce. Blend into pork; form into tiny balls.

Clean watercress thoroughly; leave whole or cut into desired length (4-8 inches/10-20 cm).

Bring stock to the boil in a saucepan. Add pork balls and boil 2 minutes until no longer pink. Add watercress and boil 3 minutes or until watercress is wilted but still crunchy. Garnish with chopped green onion and serve. **Serves 4.**

TASTE

BITTER

THREE SQUASH SOUP
Gaeng Juut Fak Saam Yang

Have fun with this fall feature by using squashes of different colours, flavours and textures. If you have time, carve them into imaginative shapes—leaves, flowers, fish, turtles—and serve in glass bowls for best effect.

1 1/2 cups	winter melon (or zucchini), skin on	375 mL
1 1/2 cups	pumpkin (or acorn squash), peeled	375 mL
1 1/2 cups	butternut squash, peeled	375 mL
5 cups	pork stock (see page 65)	1.25 L
2 tsp	fish sauce	10 mL
Pinch	ground white pepper	Pinch
1 tbsp	Crispy Fried Garlic in Oil (see page 66)	15 mL
2	green onions, finely chopped	2
5	sprigs fresh coriander	5

Leaving skin on, cut and carve winter melon into bite-sized shapes to make 1 1/2 cups (375 mL). Peel pumpkin and butternut squash; cut and carve into bite-sized shapes to make 1 1/2 cups (375 mL) each.

Bring stock to a boil in saucepan. As the squashes all cook at different rates, be sure to start with the hardest squash first (e.g., butternut), allowing 10 minutes before adding the softer squashes such as zucchini. Cook until all squash is tender.

Remove from heat. Stir in fish sauce and white pepper. Taste and adjust the seasonings if necessary.

Spoon the soup into serving bowls, dividing different squash evenly. Garnish with 1/2 tsp (2 mL) of crispy fried garlic in oil, green onions and fresh coriander. Serves 6.

TASTE
SWEET

BEAN THREAD CHICKEN NOODLE SOUP
Gaeng Juut Woon Sen Gai

What a great diet dish this is: wheat-free, egg-free, dairy-free and low in fat and calories! If you like a little colour, add some matchstick carrots and/or finely shredded cabbage.

2 cups	water	500 mL
10 oz	chicken breast, bone in	300 g
Half	cooking onion	Half
10	peppercorns	10
5 oz	bean thread noodles (3 bundles)	150 g
5 cups	chicken stock (see page 65)	1.25 L
2 tsp	fish sauce	10 mL
2	green onions, finely chopped	2
6	stalks fresh coriander, torn roughly into sprigs	6

Bring water, chicken breast, cooking onion and peppercorns to a boil in a small saucepan. Boil rapidly 20 minutes or until chicken is no longer pink inside. Remove chicken and set aside to cool. Strain liquid and discard onion and peppercorns. Discard chicken bones and skin and shred meat finely.

Soak bean thread noodles 5 minutes in hot water to cover. Drain and cut noodles with scissors into pieces suitable for a soup spoon.

Put chicken stock, chicken cooking liquid, chicken meat and noodles in a saucepan and bring to the boil. Reduce heat and simmer 5-10 minutes or until noodles are transparent and tender. Remove from heat, add fish sauce and taste for seasoning.

Serve in individual bowls garnished with chopped green onions and fresh coriander. **Serves 4-6.**

TASTE

NEARLY
NEUTRAL

BEAN CURD SOUP WITH GREEN ONIONS AND WINTER MELON
Gaeng Juut Fak Kiaw Tao Whoo

Winter melon is a pale dusty green vegetable marrow that is so large it is usually cut up and sold by the piece in Oriental markets. It stands up well to cooking and will hold its shape for re-heating. You can substitute any type of squash or vegetable marrow.

1 lb	winter melon	500 g
1 lb	firm bean curd	500 g
7	green onions	7
5 cups	pork stock (see page 65) (or vegetable stock for vegetarians)	1.25 L
1 tbsp	fish sauce, or to taste	15 mL
1/2 tsp	ground white pepper, or to taste	2 mL
6	stalks fresh coriander, torn roughly into sprigs	6
1 tbsp	Crispy Fried Garlic in Oil (see page 66), or to taste	15 mL

Peel winter melon and cut into cubes or thin crescent wedges. Drain bean curd and cut into cubes. Cut 5 green onions into short lengths and if desired, feather the ends. Finely chop remaining green onions and set aside for garnish.

Bring melon, green onions and pork stock to the boil in a heavy saucepan; cook 10-12 minutes at a gentle boil, until melon and onions are soft.

Add bean curd, cook 1 minute just to heat it through. Remove from heat. Season to taste with fish sauce and pepper.

Serve in individual bowls garnished with fresh coriander, reserved green onions and crispy fried garlic in oil. **Serves 6.**

TASTE
NEARLY
NEUTRAL

For a
*hotter soup,
bruise or crush
the chillies, for
a milder soup
leave them
whole and for
very mild soup,
use a milder
variety of
pepper and
leave whole.*

LEMON PEPPER BEEF (OR CHICKEN) SOUP
Tom Yum Nua/Tom Yum Gai

This is a more rough and ready version of the famous Lemon Shrimp Soup. It's great for inexpensive cuts of beef and tough boiling chickens.

2 lb	beef with bones (chuck, pot roast, ribs)	1 kg
8 cups	water	2 L
2	stalks fresh lemon grass, bruised and thinly sliced (or 4-6 tbsp/60-90 mL dried)	2
8	thin slices galanga (kha) root	8
2-4	wild lime (makrood) leaves, torn (not cut) in pieces	2-4
1 tbsp	fish sauce	15 mL
1 tsp	Roasted Chilli Paste (see page 114), or to taste	5 mL
6	small hot chillies	6
	Juice of 1 lime (about 2 tbsp/30 mL)	
1 tsp	ground white pepper	5 mL
1	green onion, finely chopped	1
2	stalks fresh coriander, chopped	2

Cut meat into rough chunks. Combine beef, water, lemon grass and galanga root in a saucepan, bring to the boil. Reduce heat and simmer gently about 45 minutes or until meat is tender, skimming off any foam.

Add wild lime leaves, fish sauce, chilli paste and small hot chillies. Bring to the boil. Reduce heat and simmer 15 minutes. Remove some of the beef from the bones, shred, and return to saucepan. Remove from heat and stir in lime juice and pepper. Taste and adjust seasoning if necessary.

To serve, garnish with green onion and fresh coriander. Serves 6.

Variation: Lemon Pepper Chicken Soup
To make this soup with chicken, the Thais chop the bird up roughly with a meat cleaver, smashing the bones so the marrow can run into the soup and add its sweet, rich flavour. Westerners tend to shy away from chicken bone splinters but it

TASTE
HOT
SOUR

really does make a difference in the flavour. I suggest you de-bone the chicken, smash the bones and tie them up in a piece of cheesecloth. Before adding lime juice and pepper, lift out the cheesecloth bag and discard.

SPARERIB AND BAMBOO SHOOT SOUP
Gaeng Juut Gadouk Muu

This simple soup has a rich bamboo shoot flavour, and goes well with either hot or mild dishes. Children love to eat the tender spareribs.

1	can (19 oz/540 mL) bamboo shoots in water	1
4 cups	water	1 L
1 lb	spareribs	450 g
6 tbsp	fish sauce	90 mL
1 tbsp	chopped green onion	15 mL
	Leaves from 8 stalks fresh coriander	

Drain bamboo shoots and cut into desired size. Put in a pot, cover with water and boil rapidly 15 minutes to soften and to remove some of the salty brine. (This will also turn the bamboo shoots a rich yellow colour.)

Drain bamboo shoots and discard water. Put in a heavy saucepan with water, spareribs and fish sauce. Bring to the boil and boil hard 5 minutes. Reduce heat and boil gently about 45 minutes or until spareribs are tender.

Serve garnished with green onion and fresh coriander leaves. Serves 4.

TASTE
SALTY

Winter cabbage is also known as Suey choi, Oriental cabbage or Napa cabbage. It's an elongated pale green cabbage with wide white ribs.

SEAFOOD QUENELLES SOUP
Gaeng Juut Luuk Cheen Pla

This light soup goes well with almost any meal. Try making the quenelles with different kinds of fish. I like to use three flavours of quenelles: shrimp, salmon and cod. This gives three distinct colours and tastes.

8 cups	chicken, pork or shrimp shell stock (see pages 65-66)	2 L
40	fish and shrimp quenelles (see page 120)	40
4-6 cups	coarsely chopped winter cabbage	1-1.5 L
6 tbsp	fish sauce	90 mL
2 tbsp	Crispy Fried Garlic in Oil (see page 66), or to taste	30 mL

Bring stock to boil in large saucepan. Add quenelles and boil hard 5 minutes.

Add winter cabbage and fish sauce. When soup returns to the boil and vegetables and quenelles rise to the surface, cover tightly, remove from heat and set aside until cabbage is tender, about 10 minutes.

Serve in individual bowls garnished with crispy fried garlic. **Serves 8.**

TASTE
NEARLY
NEUTRAL

FISHERMAN'S CATCH SOUP
Po Taeck

Is this a soup or a main course? The fisherman's net catches a delightful mixed harvest, which you can vary according to your taste, your budget—or what's available at the market.

12	mussels	12
4 oz	shrimp	120 g
1 tbsp	Roasted Chilli Paste (see page 114)	15 mL
6 cups	chicken stock (see page 65)	1.5 L
2	stalks lemon grass, bruised and thinly sliced	2
4	wild lime (makrood) leaves	4
4	slices galanga (kha) root	4
1 tbsp	fish sauce, or to taste	15 mL
4 oz	crab (or lobster) meat, cut in pieces	120 g
6	scallops	6
7 oz	cod, cut in pieces	200 g
12	straw mushrooms, cut in half	12
3 tbsp	lime juice (about 2 limes), or to taste	45 mL
	Leaves from 1 stalk fresh coriander	
12	small hot chillies	12
2	green onions, thinly sliced	2

Scrub mussels to remove beards and sand. Discard any that stay open. Leave shells on shrimp.

Combine chilli paste and stock in a saucepan and bring to a boil. Add lemon grass, wild lime leaves, galanga root and fish sauce; bring to a boil.

Add crab, scallops and cod; bring to boil and cook 2 minutes. Add shrimp, mussels, straw mushrooms and lime juice; return to a boil. Remove from heat as soon as mussel shells open; discard any that don't. Taste for seasonings.

Add coriander leaves, hot chillies and green onions. Serve immediately. Serves 6.

To increase the saltiness, add more fish sauce. Increase the sour sensation with the addition of lime juice. To make the soup more piquant, crush or gently pound the fresh chillies before adding them to the soup.

TASTE

HOT
SOUR

CHAPTER 6
SALADS

Thai Yum dishes are difficult to define. They aren't what Westerners expect when the word salad is mentioned. In fact, when we were devising the first menu for Bangkok Garden back in 1982, it was difficult to decide where to place these delightfully refreshing dishes on the menu or, for that matter, how to describe them.

Heartier than most Western salads, they consist of one main ingredient tossed in a tart, piquant and salty dressing with a handful of fresh herbs, shallots and shredded vegetables. The main ingredient is sometimes cooked and may even be served warm or at room temperature, the Thais having beaten the Californians to the warm salad concept by several centuries.

Salads may be eaten as snacks. Som Tam or Green Papaya Salad is a favourite of street vendors and all over Thailand you can have a dish of Som Tam shredded fresh for you and tailored exactly to your taste on virtually every street corner.

Served with sticky rice and a dish of roasted peanuts or perhaps some sheets of crisply fried Air-Dried Beef, these Yum dishes make a superb lunch.

Or serve a tart lime-flavoured Yum as the "sour" component of a taste-balanced meal: for example, with Tiger Lily Soup (see page 69), Red Curry of Chicken (see page 106), Steamed Fish (see pages 128-30) and stir-fried vegetables.

In Thailand, Yum dishes are served blisteringly hot with handfuls of bird chillies crushed into the dressing. At Bangkok Garden, we've found we can lower the chilli "bite" without interfering with the essential Thai-ness of the Yum dishes. We do this by using milder chillies.

There are many hundreds of ways to combine exotic ingredients with the basics—fresh mint, coriander, shallots, chillies, lime juice and fish sauce—to create those tart, piquant, refreshing and (if desired) hellishly hot Thai salad dishes called Yum.

I've chosen these for their popularity with Bangkok Garden customers as well as their wide range of main ingredients.

PHOTO: green papaya shredded for Green Papaya Salad (page 86)
shown with mortar and pestle, palm sugar and dried shrimp

THE ROYAL BARGE
Yum Nua

The Royal Barge carrying this hearty beef salad to your table at Bangkok Garden is a hollowed-out carved cucumber. In Thailand, this salad would be fiery-hot with tiny bird chillies; for those who prefer a milder dish, the contrast between the cool crunch of the raw vegetables and the lukewarm just-cooked meatiness of the beef makes the dish a delight even without the chillies.

The action of the fish sauce and the lime juice will cause the vegetables to wilt quickly, so don't dress the salad until you're ready to serve it.

	Leaves of 10 stalks fresh mint	
	Leaves of 1 coriander plant	
	(about 10 stalks)	
3	shallots, sliced	3
2	hot red (or green) peppers, or to taste, sliced	2
2	fresh green onions, sliced	2
1 lb	flank steak, tenderloin or other lean beef suitable for broiling	500 g
	Lettuce leaves	
	Cucumber slices	
	Carrot slices	
	Tomato wedges	
1 tbsp	roasted rice powder (see page 23)	15 mL
3-5 tbsp	fresh lime juice	45-75 mL
2-4 tbsp	fish sauce	30-60 mL
4	whole cucumbers, hollowed out	4

Combine mint and coriander leaves, shallots, hot peppers and green onions. For a hotter dish, bruise chillies before slicing.

Grill beef medium rare. Allow to cool slightly, then slice thinly against the grain.

Arrange lettuce, cucumber, carrot and tomato on a platter. Combine beef, shallot mixture, roasted rice powder, 3 tbsp (45 mL) of the lime juice and 2 tbsp (30 mL) of the fish sauce. Toss well and taste. Add lime juice and fish sauce until desired degree of sourness and saltiness is achieved. Pile into cucumber boats and serve immediately. **Serves 4.**

PHOTO: Emerald Curry (page 102-3) shown with tiny Thai eggplant (top), duck cut Oriental style, finger hot chillies (bottom) and Thai basil (bai krapow) leaves (left)

TASTE
HOT
SOUR

ROSE PETAL SALAD
Yum Dock Gulab

I had always thought of roses as temperate-climate flowers, so I was astonished to discover that Thais love to grow, display, appreciate and receive roses of all kinds.

Imagine my surprise when I discovered they like to eat them too! And not just as a flowery essence in delicate drinks and desserts—but also in savoury appetisers and salads.

If you're planning to make this charming and colourful salad with roses purchased from a florist, be sure to ask if the flowers have been sprayed with a pesticide and if in doubt, display them in a vase instead of on a dinner plate.

7 oz	chicken breast	200 g
1/2 lb	shrimp	250 g
1/2 lb	ground pork	250 g
6	cloves garlic	6
	Vegetable oil	
6	shallots	6
	Sliced fresh chillies to taste	
5 tbsp	fish sauce	75 mL
5 tbsp	fresh lime juice (3 limes)	75 mL
2 tsp	granulated sugar	10 mL
	(or other sweetener)	
	Lettuce leaves	
	Petals from 12 roses	
2 tbsp	crushed unroasted peanuts	30 mL
	(see page 22)	
6-12	sprigs fresh coriander, for garnish	6-12

Steam or boil chicken until no longer pink inside. Remove meat from bones, discard bones, fat and skin and cut meat into matchstick-sized pieces.

Peel, devein and steam shrimp about 2 minutes or until pink. Chop or leave whole.

Cook pork by putting it in a strainer and plunging into a pan of boiling water or soup stock about 3 minutes or until no longer pink, stirring once or twice. Drain and cool on paper towel.

Slice garlic very fine and fry in hot vegetable oil until brown and crisp. Drain on paper towel. Slice the shallots and cook them the same way. Slice the chillies into slivers. If a very hot salad is desired, keep seeds to sprinkle over the salad as well as the slivers.

TASTE

SWEET
HOT
SOUR

Combine fish sauce, lime juice and sweetener.

Arrange lettuce leaves on a platter or serving dish. Decorate with some of the rose petals. Combine chicken, shrimp, pork, peanuts, half of the garlic and half of the shallots with the dressing; toss well. Add the remaining rose petals, toss lightly just to mix. Mound attractively over the lettuce. Sprinkle the remaining shallots and garlic on top, and decorate with coriander and chilli slivers. **Serves 4-6.**

ELEPHANT EAR SALAD
Yum Het Hu Nuu

The secret of success in this unusual salad is to make it *à la minute*. Making it ahead will destroy the unique texture of these dark brown mushrooms.

4 oz	dry mushrooms (cloud ear, elephant ear or black fungus)	120 g
4 oz	ground pork	120 g
4 oz	shrimp, chopped	120 g
1 tbsp	chopped fresh chillies	15 mL
1 tbsp	sliced shallots	15 mL
2	large carrots, cut in matchsticks	2
1/2 cup	bean sprouts, roots removed (or shredded cabbage)	125 mL
4 tbsp	lime juice	60 mL
4 tbsp	fish sauce	60 mL
4	stalks fresh coriander, coarsely chopped	4
4	green onions, finely chopped	4
	Lettuce leaves	

Soak mushrooms for 10 minutes in lukewarm water. Drain, rinse well to remove all sand, and dry off excess moisture. Steam or boil pork and shrimp until pork is no longer pink; drain.

In bowl, combine mushrooms, pork, shrimp, chillies, shallots, carrots, bean sprouts, lime juice, fish sauce, coriander and green onions. Taste for seasonings and adjust if necessary.

Serve immediately on individual plates on a bed of lettuce. **Serves 4.**

TASTE
SOUR

GREEN PAPAYA SALAD
Som Tam

Street vendors all over Thailand custom-blend this tasty salad exactly to your specifications. Papayas fruit all year round, and papaya trees grow from seed to fruit in only 6 months, so wherever there's an enterprising vendor with a grater and a mortar, there's Som Tam. This dish originates in the North, and is a favourite mid-afternoon snack. You can also serve it as a salad, especially with rich curry dishes, or as a light meal with sticky rice and Air-Dried Beef (see page 54).

In Thailand, Som Tam is incendiary; make this Thai-hot by adding a handful of tiny hot chillies, or tone it down by substituting milder chillies for the hot ones. For a richer, slightly fishy taste, add some salted crab or 1-2 teaspoons (5-10 mL) shrimp paste.

2	cloves garlic	2
2	hot red chillies	2
4 tbsp	dried shrimp	60 mL
4 tbsp	unroasted peanuts (see page 22)	60 mL
2	green beans	2
2 tbsp	lime juice	30 mL
2 tbsp	fish sauce	30 mL
2 tsp	palm sugar	10 mL
2 cups	shredded peeled green papaya	500 mL
4	cherry tomatoes, sliced or	4
2	carrots, grated	2

In a mortar, pound garlic and chillies. Add dried shrimp and peanuts; pound until in small pieces. Slice green beans in 3/4-inch (2 cm) pieces, add to mortar and pound. Combine lime juice, fish sauce and palm sugar and stir until sugar has dissolved. To serve, combine papaya, tomatoes or carrots and contents of mortar and mix well. Top with dressing. **Serves 2-4.**

T
A
S
T
E
HOT
SOUR

SHREDDING PAPAYA

To shred papaya Thai style, hold the peeled fruit in your left hand (assuming you are right handed) and with a meat cleaver in your right hand, make a series of parallel cuts 5 mm (1/4 inch) deep, close together, all around the papaya. Thais can do this quickly by keeping up a steady chopping rhythm, chop chop chop chop TURN, chop chop chop chop TURN. This takes a steady eye and hand. It's worth taking the time to learn this skill.

When the surface of the papaya is covered with parallel gashes, take a paring knife and cut down from top to bottom, about 5 mm deep, to create long smooth shreds. Keep paring until there are no more cuts, then repeat the process, making a new set of cuts with the meat cleaver.

See photo opposite page 82.

Glass noodles,
also known as
bean thread,
mung bean or
cellophane noo-
dles, are usually
sold in 50 g
bundles, 8 or 10
bundles to a
package.

GLASS NOODLE SALAD
Yum Woon Sen

We find this dish meets a wide variety of dietary needs—it's low-calorie, low in simple starches, wheat-free, low in cholesterol (lower still if you leave out the shrimp) and as hot or as mild as you care to make it.

Once you've made it a few times, I'm sure you'll feel comfortable playing with the ingredients and making it into your own signature salad.

2 oz	cloud ear mushrooms	50 g
1/2 lb	bean thread noodles (5 bundles)	250 g
2 tbsp	lime juice	30 mL
4 oz	small shrimp	120 g
4 oz	ground pork	120 g
	(or ground chicken breast)	
2 tbsp	dried shrimp, or to taste	30 mL
1	shallot, sliced	1
2 tbsp	fish sauce	30 mL
2	green onions, sliced diagonally	2
	in 2-inch/5 cm slivers	
2	fresh bird chillies, or to taste,	2
	bruised then sliced	
10	stems fresh coriander, torn roughly	10
	Fructose (or other sweetener) (optional)	
	Fresh mint and Thai basil leaves	
	from about 10 sprigs	

Garnish

	Lettuce	
1	carrot, shredded	1
2	green onions, chopped	2
2	red chillies, chopped	2

Soak mushrooms in lukewarm water for 20 minutes. Drain and rinse to remove all grit and sand. Soak noodles in lukewarm water for 10 minutes or until tender. Drain and toss with lime juice. Steam shrimp until pink. Steam pork or chicken until no longer pink. Roast or deep-fry dried shrimp.

In bowl, combine noodles, steamed and roasted shrimp, pork, shallot, fish sauce, mushrooms, green onions, chillies, coriander, fructose if desired, mint and basil leaves; toss to mix.

TASTE
SOUR

Arrange noodle mixture on a lettuce bed. Garnish with carrot, onion and chillies. **Serves 4-6.**

CITRONELLA SHRIMP SALAD
Pla Kung

For this salad to taste as fresh and lemony as it would if prepared on the Gulf of Siam, be sure to start with uncooked shrimp and bruise the lemon grass stalks thoroughly before slicing them to ensure maximum release of flavour. Lemon grass stalks are generally tough, even when quite young, so choose four of the tenderest you can find.

14 oz	raw salad shrimp	400 g
4	stalks lemon grass	4
4 tbsp	lime juice	60 mL
2 tbsp	fish sauce	30 mL
1 tsp	fructose (or other sweetener)	5 mL
1	coriander plant	1
10	stalks fresh mint	10
4	shallots	4
2	hot red peppers, or to taste	2
2	green onions	2

In sieve or wire basket, cook shrimp until just pink by plunging into a pot of rapidly boiling shrimp shell stock (see page 66) or water. Bruise lemon grass well, slice *very* thinly into rounds and place in bowl.

Combine lime juice, fish sauce and fructose and pour over lemon grass. Set aside to allow flavours to blend.

Remove root from coriander plant and set aside for use in another dish. Remove leaves from stalks and keep whole; chop stalks coarsely. Remove leaves from mint and discard stalks. Set aside a handful of the mint and coriander leaves for garnish. Slice shallots thinly in rounds.

Pound hot peppers to release the oils, then chop finely. Cut green onion tops for garnish. Then cut white stalks in 4 pieces lengthwise, then into 1-inch (2.5 cm) lengths.

Ten minutes before serving, combine shrimp with lemon grass mixture and allow to stand.

To serve, combine with remaining ingredients and toss well. Mound on a plate and garnish with mint and coriander leaves and green onion tops. **Serves 4.**

Don't leave lemon grass mixture much longer than 10 minutes or the lime juice will make the shrimp mushy.

Coriander roots freeze well; keep a bag in your freezer for saving coriander roots until you have enough for a curry paste.

T
A
S
T
E
HOT
SOUR

TUNA YUM SALAD
Yum Pla Ob

It's easy to throw this hot and salty salad together for a quick snack or lunch dish. For a milder salad, do not reduce the number of chillies but use a milder type of chilli instead. Serve with steamed rice, sticky rice or rice crackers.

	Juice of 2 limes	
2-4 tbsp	fish sauce	30-60 mL
2 tsp	fructose (or other sweetener)	10 mL
4	small hot bird chillies, or to taste	4
2	green onions	2
4	stalks fresh coriander	4
2	shallots	2
2	cans (6.5-7 oz/180-200 g) whole tuna, water packed	2
8	lettuce leaves (Romaine or leaf)	8
	Handful fresh mint leaves (optional)	

In a bowl, combine lime juice, fish sauce and fructose and stir until fructose dissolves. Bruise chillies and slice into rounds.

Chop green onions fine. Remove leaves from coriander and set aside for garnish. Chop stalks. Slice shallots thinly. Drain tuna and break up slightly. Combine all ingredients in bowl with lime juice mixture. Toss.

Arrange on a bed of lettuce, sprinkle with coriander leaves, garnish with mint if desired, and serve immediately. **Serves 2-4.**

Do not finish yum dishes ahead of time. The dressing will cause everything to wilt. To prepare ahead, keep dressing separate and toss into tuna mixture just before carrying it to the table.

TASTE

HOT
SOUR
SALTY

CRISPY FISH SALAD
Yum Pla Dook Foo

In Thailand, catfish is favoured for this dish. You can substitute other fish as available.

2 lb	firm-fleshed fish	1 kg
2-3 cups	light vegetable oil for deep-frying	500-750 mL
	Fish head and tail, if desired	
2	shallots	2
10-20	chillies, to taste	10-20
Half	sweet red pepper	Half
	Fresh coriander sprigs	
4 tbsp	lime juice	60 mL
3 tbsp	fish sauce	45 mL
5 tbsp	fructose	75 mL
	Lettuce	

Bake, steam or barbecue fish. Remove skin and bones and flake flesh into a measuring cup.

Heat vegetable oil in a wok until beginning to smoke. Add fish flakes and deep-fry about 5 minutes, turning occasionally with spatula or slotted spoon. Fold the fish into itself as though it were an omelette, to make several large blocks of fish flakes. When fish is crispy and brown, remove and drain on paper towel. Some varieties of fish will clump together when deep-fried this way; others will hang loose. If you have the fish head and tail, fry them in the hot oil until crispy.

Slice shallots, chillies and sweet pepper. Wash and dry coriander.

To make dressing, combine lime juice, fish sauce and fructose and stir until fructose has dissolved.

To serve, arrange crispy fish on a bed of lettuce. If using, put fish head at one end and the tail at the other end of the cooked fish. Sprinkle with sliced shallots and chillies. Garnish with sweet pepper slices and coriander sprigs. Pour dressing over. Serve at once. Eat with steamed rice or sticky rice and clear soup (Gaeng Juut). **Serves 4-6.**

TASTE

SALTY
SOUR
HOT
SWEET

BOILED EGG SALAD
Yum Khaay Tom

The smokey flavour of the barbecued chillies, garlic and shallots plays so well off the blandness of the boiled eggs! It's a deceptively simple dish that will really grab your attention. The secret of this salad is to cook the eggs until the whites are completely hard but the yolks are still bright yellow-orange and moist (but not runny).

4	eggs	4
2	red chillies	2
2	green chillies	2
2	shallots	2
5	large cloves garlic	5
3 tbsp	fish sauce	45 mL
4 tbsp	lime juice	60 mL
5 tbsp	fructose	75 mL
4-6	lettuce leaves	4-6
4	stalks fresh coriander	4

Put the eggs into a pot of boiling water and boil hard exactly 5 minutes. Plunge eggs at once into cold water to stop the cooking process. Peel and set aside.

Thread the red and green chillies, shallots and garlic onto skewers and barbecue until charred and vegetables are soft. Remove skins and cut into quarters or eighths.

Combine fish sauce, lime juice and fructose and stir until fructose dissolves.

Arrange lettuce on a serving plate. Cut eggs in half and put on lettuce. Sprinkle barbecued vegetables over eggs and garnish with coriander stalks. Pour dressing over all. Serve with rice or sticky rice and a clear soup (Gaeng Juut). **Serves 4.**

TASTE

BITTER
SWEET
SOUR
HOT
SALTY

BBQ EGGPLANT SALAD
Yum Makua Yaaw Yang

The long green or purple eggplants give the best presentation in this dish, but you can try it with other eggplants or even other vegetables.

You're going to love the mellow, smokey flavour of this salad that hits all five of the taste centres at once.

5	large cloves garlic	5
2	shallots	2
4	long eggplants	4
4	finger-hot chillies	4
	Lettuce	
2 tbsp	dried shrimp	30 mL
3 tbsp	fructose	45 mL
3 tbsp	fish sauce	45 mL
3 tbsp	lime juice	45 mL
	Green onion tops	
	Fresh coriander sprigs	

Thread the garlic cloves and shallots on bamboo skewers. Barbecue along with eggplants and chillies until charred. Let stand until cool enough to handle; peel. Leave the eggplants whole; lay on a bed of lettuce on an oval serving dish and cut lengthwise once, then crosswise into 2 1/2-inch (6 cm) pieces.

Chop garlic roughly. Slice shallots and chillies. Sprinkle over eggplants. Pound dried shrimp into shreds and sprinkle over.

Combine fructose, fish sauce and lime juice and stir until fructose dissolves. Pour over eggplants. Garnish with green onion tops and coriander sprigs. Do not dress salad until ready to serve. Serves 4.

If you don't have a barbecue or gas grill, you can char the vegetables on the burner of your electric stove and finish cooking 10 minutes in a moderate oven or 3 minutes in a microwave.

TASTE

BITTER
SWEET
SOUR
HOT
SALTY

GRAPEFRUIT SALAD
Yum Som Oh

It's worth the time and effort it takes to prepare this unusual salad. If you find a red or pink grapefruit, the effect is even more spectacular. For larger quantities, you might want to use two different colours of grapefruit.

In Thailand, a giant variety called Pomelo is used. It has a milder flavour and can sometimes be found in grocery stores, particularly on the west coast. I find I prefer the more assertive flavour of North American grapefruit.

1	large grapefruit	1
2 tbsp	unsweetened dried coconut	30 mL
1 tbsp	light vegetable oil	15 mL
2	shallots, sliced	2
2 tbsp	dried shrimp	30 mL
1/2 cup	small raw salad shrimp	125 mL
3 tbsp	fructose	45 mL
3 tbsp	fish sauce	45 mL
3 tbsp	lime juice	45 mL
2 tbsp	chopped unroasted cashews	30 mL
	Lettuce	
4	sprigs fresh coriander	4
	Green onion tops, chopped	
2	red chillies, slivered	2

Peel grapefruit. Peel and discard the membrane from each individual section.

Heat a clean, dry wok and toast coconut by stirring quickly until it turns golden brown—about 1 minute. Set aside.

Heat oil in a small pot or wok. Fry shallots until deep toasty brown. Drain on paper towel.

Pound dried shrimp in a mortar until shredded. Steam or boil salad shrimp 2-3 minutes until just pink.

Combine fructose, fish sauce and lime juice and stir until fructose dissolves. Put in a cruet; it's best to dress this salad at the table.

To serve, combine grapefruit, toasted coconut, salad shrimp and cashews, and toss lightly. Turn onto a bed of lettuce on serving plate. Sprinkle with dried shrimp and fried shallot slices and garnish with coriander sprigs, green onion tops and slivered chillies. Pour the dressing over the salad at the table. Serves 4.

It is easier to remove the grapefruit membranes if you leave individual segments to dry out for a few hours, or even overnight.

T
A
S
T
E

BITTER

GRILLED BANANA PEPPER SALAD
Yum Prik Youack

Here's an intriguing dish that Westerners probably wouldn't call salad, as everything in it is cooked. I like it because it treats hot peppers as a vegetable rather than a flavouring. Consequently, it's just loaded with Vitamin C! You'll notice the coconut cream acts to temper the bite of the chillies.

5	large banana peppers	5
1-2	shallots	1-2
1 tbsp	light vegetable oil	15 mL
7 oz	small raw salad shrimp	200 g
7 oz	pork tenderloin	200 g
2 tbsp	fish sauce	30 mL
3 tbsp	lime juice	45 mL
2 tsp	fructose	10 mL
2 tbsp	coconut cream	30 mL
8	sprigs fresh coriander, for garnish	8

Barbecue banana peppers until soft and charred. Cool, then remove skins and seeds and cut into large chunks. Slice shallots and deep-fry in hot oil until dark golden brown. Drain on paper towel.

Scald shrimp in boiling water just until pink. Steam pork tenderloin until no longer pink, cool and cut into thin slices or matchsticks.

In bowl, combine fish sauce, lime juice and fructose and stir well until fructose has dissolved. Add banana peppers, shrimp and pork and toss well.

Mound on a serving dish, drizzle with coconut cream. Sprinkle with crispy fried shallots and decorate with fresh coriander sprigs. Serve immediately.

Makes a small salad, but because it's hot it will likely serve 4.

TASTE
HOT

MOCK MANGO SALAD
Yum Appen

No one believed we could find a substitute for the tart, fresh and slightly resiny taste of the hard green mangoes that go into one of Thailand's most beloved salads.

Then we discovered the answer had been under our noses all along—home-grown Granny Smith or Mutsue apples from BC or the Niagara Peninsula!

The secret is in the slicing. You *must* shred the apples Thai-style. Follow the directions for shredding green papaya (see page 87) and you'll marvel at how close this salad comes to the real thing.

1/2 lb	chicken breast	250 g
5 oz	unroasted peanuts	150 g
5 oz	dried shrimp	150 g
5	shallots	5
1/2 cup	light vegetable oil, for deep-frying	125 mL
2	large tart green apples, shredded Thai-style	2
1/2 cup	coconut cream	125 mL
4	chillies (or powdered chillies to taste)	4
4 tbsp	lime juice	60 mL
4 tbsp	fish sauce	60 mL
1 tbsp	fructose	15 mL
	Lettuce	
	Fresh coriander sprigs	

Steam or boil chicken breast until no longer pink inside. Cool, then slice across the grain. Pound peanuts roughly.

Pound dried shrimp in a mortar until shredded. Slice shallots and deep-fry in hot oil until golden brown. Drain on a paper towel and set aside for garnish.

Combine chicken, apples, peanuts, dried shrimp, coconut cream and chillies and toss. Combine lime juice, fish sauce and fructose and stir until fructose has dissolved. Add to apple mixture and toss.

Mound on a bed of lettuce on serving plate. Sprinkle with toasted shallots, garnish with coriander and serve immediately. Serves 4-6.

If you have the time, it's worth the extra effort to prepare fresh coconut cream (page 100) rather than using the canned variety. You'll notice the difference!

TASTE
SOUR

CHAPTER 7
THAI CURRIES

· · · · · · · · · · · ·

What makes a Thai curry Thai? How does it differ from an East or West Indian or an Indonesian curry?

The foundation is an essential combination of ingredients that gives a truly Thai flavour to all Thai foods, curried or otherwise: fish sauce, pepper, garlic and fresh coriander root pounded together. Most Thai curries start with these basics, along with a great many fresh leaves, roots and stems. Some of these are found only in Southeast Asia.

Curries from most other parts of the world are made principally from spice seeds, dried and roasted before being pounded together. Thai curries feature mostly fresh ingredients—aromatic roots of plants of the ginger family, citrus leaves and peel, the lemon-tasting stalks of lemon grass, peppers and onions of various kinds.

A common belief is that all Thai food is hot, and that the "heat" comes entirely from the world's hottest chilli peppers, grown in Thailand and (yes—we admit it!) used liberally in many Thai dishes. Actually, the chilli pepper is a relative newcomer to the Asian cookery scene. It was introduced into Thailand, India and Indonesia by Portuguese traders at the beginning of the 16th century. The first record of chilli peppers being grown in Thailand appears in 1507, in the Northern province of Sukhothai.

Prior to the introduction of the chilli pepper in the early 1600s, Thais created the fire in their curries with the berries of the pepper vine, *Piper nigrum*. Today we know this as ordinary table pepper.

There are five or six basic curry pastes in general use today, and these form the basis for dozens of exotic curries with tastes ranging from sweet and hot to tangy and rich. Most Thai households buy their curry pastes in the market, leaving it to the experts to pound and blend the 15-30 different ingredients required for each paste.

At Bangkok Garden, we have our curry pastes custom blended to our specifications in Bangkok and air-freighted regularly to Toronto. When we opened the restaurant, this was essential because there were six or seven ingredients we had trouble obtaining regularly. As more Southeast Asians make their culinary wishes known in North America, this number has decreased to one or two.

It is now quite possible, with a little perseverance, to obtain the ingredients required for the curry paste recipes given in this chapter. Once made, these pastes will keep perfectly in the refrigerator for months; longer in the freezer. It's best to make a largish quantity whenever you assemble the vital components, and save the unused portion for later meals. Once you've got the paste, making the curry is a snap so don't overlook these recipes just because they seem complicated. One day of strenuous effort can yield many quick and delightful Thai meals.

All of these recipes were made and tested with ingredients purchased at retail shops in Toronto.

A Word About Bones

Most Oriental cooks shatter the bones of poultry as they cut it up for curry. This releases the bone marrow and gives the curry a meatier flavour.

Most Westerners, however, find it difficult to deal with the resulting bone splinters in their curry. We learned early on that Bangkok Garden customers preferred their curry boneless and skinless, and we now make all our chicken curries with boneless chicken breast.

But that's for the restaurant. If you're making curry at home there are two ways to get the bones-in flavour without ending up with a little pile of splinters on your plate.

The first is to cut the chicken (or duck) European-style. This gives you larger pieces, but leaves the bones whole. The second method is to remove the bones, crack them, tie them securely in a cheesecloth bag, and add to the curry at the beginning of the cooking process. Before serving, lift out the bone bag and discard.

A Word About Oil

A good Thai curry has a rich layer of oil shimmering on top. This is not the result of a super-fatty fowl or cut of meat—it's the natural oil of the coconut that has separated out during the lengthy stewing process.

Thais regard this as essential. Some Westerners are horrified at the sight of all that fat; even when they discover it's not "grease" they are repelled by it. Skim the coconut oil off if you must, but be warned that you'll never get it all and as long as the curry remains in the cooking pot or serving dish, oil will continue to separate out from the coconut milk.

If you really can't stand the sight of that lovely oil, stick to the drier curries such as Panang (see page 113).

You can't do it in a food processor: A curry paste must be pounded, not chopped fine in a blender or food processor. Garlic must be pounded in order to release its special flavour; other ingredients carry their flavours in essential oils that only pounding will release. A blender merely cuts the ingredients into small pieces, leaving the oils still locked inside. Only hard, rhythmic pounding in the traditional fashion will release the oils into the curry paste. You can shorten the process considerably by blending or grinding first, then pounding the resulting paste vigorously by hand for 3-5 minutes.

*If possible,
use freshly
grated meat
from mature
coconuts.
If using dried
coconut instead
of fresh, make
sure it is
unsweetened.*

COCONUT MILK AND COCONUT CREAM
Thin and Thick Coconut Milk
Nam Gati and Hua Gati

Coconut milk is the liquid used in all curries; coconut cream provides oil for the initial sauteeing of the meat, adds a silky richness in the finishing of a dish, and is also used extensively in desserts.

To prepare a fresh coconut, use a hammer and small screwdriver or an awl to pierce two of the three weak spots or "eyes," and drain the coconut water through the holes.

With a hammer or the blunt edge of a heavy knife, tap the coconut hard about 1/3 down from the eyes, while slowly turning it. When you reach the coconut's fault line, you will hear a faint cracking sound. Continue tapping on the fault line until the coconut splits in two.

The halves can then be broken into pieces with a hammer. Use a knife to remove the white meat from the shell.

One mature supermarket coconut will yield approximately 2 cups (500 mL) grated coconut meat.

8 cups	water (milk for a richer curry)	2 L
5 cups	freshly grated (or dried	1.25 L
	unsweetened shredded) coconut	

Bring water to a full boil (or scald milk), add coconut, stir until coconut is heated through, then remove from heat. Cover and let stand until at room temperature.

Strain through a sieve. Wrap the strained coconut in a tea towel and squeeze to remove as much of the milk as possible. Discard coconut. Refrigerate liquid until a layer of thick cream forms at the top. Skim this cream and store separately.

Makes about 3/4 cup (175 mL) cream and 4-5 cups (1-1.25 L) milk.

Although fresh coconut milk and cream undoubtedly produce the best results, you can save a lot of time and effort with the canned variety. To separate the cream and the milk, refrigerate cans a few hours before opening. The cream will solidify, enabling you to lift it out with a spoon. (For further discussion, see page 13.)

In this chapter, I have assumed you'll be using cans. If making up fresh coconut milk and cream, assume 1 can equals 2 cups (500 mL) fresh milk and 4 tbsp (60 mL) cream.

GREEN CURRY PASTE
Krung Gaeng Keo Waan

1 tsp	black peppercorns	5 mL
4	fresh coriander roots	4
1 tbsp	fish sauce	15 mL
1 tsp	shrimp paste (kapi)	5 mL
1 tbsp	vegetable oil	15 mL
4-8	small green chillies, to taste	4-8
8	cloves garlic (2 tbsp/30 mL chopped)	8
2 tbsp	chopped galanga (kha) root (about 2 in/5 cm)	30 mL
2	stalks lemon grass	2
2	wild lime (makrood) leaves (or 2 tbsp/30 mL grated lime zest)	2
2 tbsp	chopped shallots	30 mL

Grind peppercorns in spice or coffee grinder. Pound coriander roots in a mortar.

Blend fish sauce, shrimp paste, oil, chillies, garlic, galanga root, lemon grass, wild lime leaves and shallots in a mortar or food processor. Add peppercorns and coriander roots and pound or blend to a smooth paste. If using a food processor, finish by pounding vigorously 3-5 minutes in a mortar to release essential oils. Add more oil if necessary. **Makes 6-8 tbsp (90-120 mL).**

To increase the "bite," increase number of fresh chillies and black peppercorns used.

This paste can be stored many months, covered, in a cool place.

EMERALD CURRY OF BEEF
Gaeng Keo Waan Nua

A powerful and potent curry resplendent with garlic and fresh Thai basil, this is one of Thailand's favourites. It's hot—fresh whole finger chillies are customarily cooked along with the eggplant as a vegetable.

Thais like to eat this curry with beef, chicken or fish quenelles. It is a staple on any hotel menu and can be purchased ready prepared at any street market.

2	cans (19 oz/540 mL each) coconut milk	2
5 tbsp	Green Curry Paste (see page 101)	75 mL
1 lb	beef, cubed (or cut into strips)	500 g
8-10	wild lime (makrood) leaves, roughly torn in quarters	8-10
1 tsp	salt	5 mL
2 tbsp	fish sauce	30 mL
2 cups	cubed eggplant (or 1 cup/250 mL baby Thai eggplant)	500 mL
1 tbsp	fructose (or other sweetener), or to taste	15 mL

Garnish

3	chillies, slivered	3
10	fresh Thai basil leaves	10
2 tbsp	fresh coriander leaves (optional)	30 mL

Spoon 3 tbsp (45 mL) of the solidified coconut cream into a wok or a very heavy-bottomed pan. Set aside any remaining cream. Cook, stirring, over medium heat until the cream boils and the coconut oil begins to separate and rise to the surface.

Add the green curry paste, increase heat slightly, and continue cooking for approximately 5 minutes or until the mixture begins to change colour and give off a strong aromatic spicy smell. Increase heat, add the beef pieces, stir well and cook 5 minutes. Add coconut milk, stir until curry begins to bubble, reduce heat to low, cover and continue cooking 15 minutes, stirring occasionally. Add wild lime leaves, salt and fish sauce and bring to boil. Reduce heat to simmer and continue cooking, uncovered, about 30 minutes or until the beef is tender.

A good Thai curry should have a generous layer of coconut oil shimmering on top. Do not skim this unless you think the amount of oil in the dish is excessive.

TASTE

SWEET
HOT
SALTY

Add eggplant, fructose and remaining coconut cream (if any); cook for 10 minutes. Adjust seasonings: add more fish sauce to increase saltiness, fructose to tone down the heat.

To serve, sprinkle with chillies, basil and coriander leaves (if using). **Serves 4-6.**

Variation: For **Emerald Curry of Duck**, substitute a 3 lb (1.5 kg) roasting duck for the beef and omit eggplant. Wash duck, pat dry and remove large pieces of fat and excess skin. Cut into bite-sized pieces. Before adding coconut milk, check amount of fat and skim off excess if necessary.

A Thai-Chinese version of this dish calls for barbecued duck. Buy the duck already barbecued from a Chinese butcher, and have him cut it up. Add coconut milk directly after stirring duck pieces and curry mixture together and cook 20 minutes before adding fructose and remaining coconut cream. **Serves 4-6.**

If using tiny Thai eggplant, bruise before adding to assist in the cooking process.

RED CURRY PASTE
Krung Gaeng Deng

Adjust the heat of this potent curry paste by adjusting the amount of chilli *seeds* you put into it. If you remove all the seeds from the dried chillies, the curry paste will remain red but will be considerably milder than when the seeds are left in. If you want to cut down on dried chillies altogether, add some red paprika to maintain this paste's rich red colour.

To make this paste hotter, increase the amount of black pepper as well as dried chillies. And remember, you can always strengthen the "kick" of a curry by adding fresh chillies at the beginning of the cooking process!

1 tbsp	coriander seed	15 mL
1 tsp	cumin seed	5 mL
1/2 cup	chopped shallots	125 mL
1/2 cup	chopped garlic	125 mL
6	stalks lemon grass, chopped	6
6	fresh coriander roots	6
1 tbsp	chopped galanga (kha) root	15 mL
1 tsp	grated wild lime (makrood) peel	5 mL
1 tsp	coarsely ground black pepper	5 mL
1/2 tsp	ground mace	2 mL
1/2 tsp	ground nutmeg	2 mL
20	dried red chillies	20
2 tbsp	shrimp paste (kapi)	30 mL
1 tbsp	fish sauce	15 mL

Roast coriander and cumin seeds by stir-frying them in a dry wok over high heat about 1 minute. In a mortar or food processor, pound together roasted coriander and cumin seeds, shallots, garlic, lemon grass, coriander roots, galanga root, wild lime peel, black pepper, mace, nutmeg, red chillies, shrimp paste and fish sauce until thoroughly blended and smooth. If necessary, add a little vegetable oil to help keep the mixture moving. When ingredients are thoroughly blended, pound again about 2 minutes in a mortar to release the flavour oils.

Store in a tightly covered container in the refrigerator. Will keep for months. **Makes about 12 tbsp (180 mL).**

JUNGLE CURRY
Gaeng Pa

This is a rough-and-ready, strongly flavoured curry that was originally developed for use with wild boar meat. It doesn't have any culinary polish—the presentation is meant to suggest it was chopped up with a crude knife and boiled up in the jungle.

Well, it's just as good in the urban jungle, and this is one of the few Thai dishes where it's OK to be crude. Hack up your ingredients and enjoy!

1 lb	pork loin	500 g
1/2 lb	krachai root	250 g
3 tbsp	vegetable oil	45 mL
2 tbsp	Red Curry Paste (see page 104)	30 mL
2 cups	water	500 mL
1	can (19 oz/540 mL) bamboo shoots	1
1/2 lb	green beans	250 g
1/2 lb	eggplant, preferably tiny round Thai ones	250 g
4 tbsp	fish sauce	60 mL
1 tsp	fructose	5mL
5-10	fresh Thai basil leaves	5-10

Cut pork loin into 1/2-inch (1 cm) thick slices. Cut krachai root roughly in matchsticks.

Heat oil in a heavy-bottomed pot or wok. Add curry paste and stir-fry 5 minutes, until the curry paste begins to give off a strong smell. Add 1/2 cup (125 mL) of the water, bring to the boil. Add pork loin and cook until meat turns white. Add krachai. Continue boiling, adding water 1/2 cup (125 mL) at a time at 10-minute intervals, for 30 minutes.

Meanwhile, drain bamboo shoots, cut roughly and boil 10 minutes in enough water to cover. Drain and discard water. Add bamboo shoots to curry. Boil gently 10 minutes.

Add beans, eggplant and some more water if necessary. Bring to the boil 10 minutes, until beans are tender. Add fish sauce and fructose and adjust taste.

Garnish with fresh basil leaves. **Serves 4-6.**

For a genuine jungle flavour you really need to use krachai root, but if it's unavailable, use fresh ginger root. The taste won't be the same, but you'll get a good curry.

If tiny Thai eggplants are not available substitute available eggplant and chop roughly.

TASTE
SALTY

RED CURRY OF CHICKEN
Gaeng Ped Gai

This very popular curry can also be made with fish, pork or other fowl. Use any type of eggplant you like, or vary the taste slightly by using other vegetables that will hold their shape during the cooking process: bamboo shoots, baby corn, green beans. Thais prefer this curry to be more liquid, and may use up to double the amount of coconut milk recommended. Feel free to adjust according to your taste.

1	can (19 oz/540 mL) coconut milk	1
2 tbsp	Red Curry Paste (see page 104)	30 mL
1 1/3 lb	chicken, cut in bite-sized pieces	600 g
6	wild lime (makrood) leaves, torn roughly	6
1	eggplant, cut in cubes	1
4	whole fresh red chillies, or to taste	4
4	whole fresh green chillies, or to taste	4
12	fresh Thai basil leaves	12

Spoon 3 tbsp (45 mL) of the solidified coconut cream into a heavy-bottomed saucepan or stewing pot. Stir-fry curry paste over medium heat 5 minutes. Raise heat, add chicken and continue cooking over high heat until chicken is browned, about 10 minutes. Add coconut milk, bring to the boil, reduce heat and simmer 15 minutes.

Add wild lime leaves and eggplant and simmer 10 minutes. Garnish with whole fresh red and green chillies and basil leaves. Serves 4.

Use whatever part of the chicken you prefer, cut into bite-sized pieces. Some people prefer to use boneless chicken but this will result in a less flavourful curry. Thai cooks often smash the bones to release the marrow for greater flavour.

TASTE

HOT
SALTY

"ORANGE" CURRY OF SHRIMP
Gaeng Som Kung

Is this dish a soup or a curry? Thais would say it's a curry, and serve it in a serving dish along with the other main-course entrées. To eat it this way, spoon it over rice even though it may seem runny.

Most Westerners prefer to serve and eat this in small individual bowls. Either way, it's a taste sensation!

1 1/2 cups	chopped vegetables* (your favourite ones)	375 mL
3 cups	shrimp shell stock (see page 66)	750 mL
2 tbsp	Red Curry Paste (see page 104)	30 mL
1/2 lb	shrimp, peeled	250 g
2 tbsp	fish sauce	30 mL
4 tbsp	tamarind puree	60 mL
2 tbsp	lemon (or lime) juice	30 mL
2 tsp	fructose (or other sweetener), or to taste	10 mL

*We use a mixture of cabbage, carrots, green beans, cooking onions and tomatoes.

Cook vegetables in shrimp shell stock until nearly tender. Remove and set aside.

Add curry paste to stock, mix well and bring to a boil. Add shrimp and simmer 1-2 minutes, until shrimp are pink. Add the vegetables, fish sauce and tamarind puree, bring to a boil, and simmer for an additional 3 minutes. Add lime juice, and fructose as desired. Taste, and adjust the seasonings for sour, hot and sweet, in that order. **Makes 4 small or 2 generous servings.**

For a more strongly flavoured soup/curry, add 1 teaspoon (5 mL) or more of shrimp paste (kapi), to taste.

At home, we often make this curry with canned tuna instead of shrimp. Use solid white tuna packed in water for best results.

TASTE
HOT
SOUR

KUA CURRY PASTE
Krung Gaeng Kua

You may grind the ingredients in a food processor, but finish off with 3-5 minutes of vigorous hand pounding to release all the flavours.

This curry paste should be a red colour; if a milder paste is desired, remove the seeds from the chillies before pounding into the paste.

10	dried red chillies	10
4 tbsp	chopped garlic	60 mL
4 tbsp	chopped shallots	60 mL
2 tbsp	chopped lemon grass (1 stalk)	30 mL
1/2 tsp	grated wild lime (makrood) peel	2 mL
1 tbsp	grated galanga (kha) root	15 mL
2	fresh coriander roots	2
1 tbsp	grated krachai root	15 mL
1/2 tsp	coarsely ground black pepper	2 mL
1 1/2 tsp	fish sauce	7 mL

Using mortar and pestle, pound together dried red chillies, garlic, shallots, lemon grass, wild lime peel, galanga root, coriander roots, krachai root, black pepper and fish sauce until a fine paste.
Makes about 12 tbsp (180 mL).

RED CURRY OF PUMPKIN WITH BEEF
Gaeng Ped Nua Fak Thong

Here's a terrific fall and winter dish using the season's squash harvest. Be sure to serve it in a hollowed-out pumpkin or squash for maximum effect.

1	can (14 oz/398 mL) coconut milk	1
1 lb	beef tenderloin, thinly sliced	500 g
2 tbsp	Kua Curry Paste	30 mL
	(see page opposite)	
1 cup	water	250 mL
12 oz	pumpkin, peeled and chopped	350 g
4 tbsp	fish sauce	60 mL
1 tbsp	fructose	15 mL

Garnish

30	fresh Thai basil leaves	30
2	red finger-hot chillies, sliced diagonally	2

Remove coagulated thick cream from coconut milk with a spoon and set aside. Pour the liquid (thin) coconut milk into a heavy saucepan. Bring to the boil over high heat. Add sliced beef, return to the boil. Reduce heat and simmer gently 20 minutes or until beef is tender.

In a separate saucepan, melt reserved thick coconut cream. Fry the Kua Curry Paste over medium heat 5 minutes. Add 4 tablespoons (60 mL) of the coconut milk that the beef was boiled in. Boil another 5 minutes, then add beef and coconut milk, plus 1 cup (250 mL) water (slosh it around in the coconut milk can to get the last of the coconut milk). Bring to the boil. (Dish can be prepared to this point and refrigerated until ready to serve.)

Add pumpkin and boil 5 minutes, or until pumpkin is tender but not mushy. Add fish sauce and fructose. Taste for seasoning.

Just before serving, sprinkle with Thai basil leaves and sliced chillies. **Serves 4.**

TASTE
HOT

You can
also use Red
Curry Paste
instead of Kua
Curry Paste for
this dish.

RED CURRY OF WINTER MELON WITH PORK
Gaeng Kua Fak Kiaw

Winter melon is a large pale dusty green marrow that is generally cut up and sold in chunks.

This curry actually improves with age: if you leave it overnight, the winter melon absorbs the curry flavours and tastes wonderfully tangy. You'll be pleased to know you can use fresh or dried wild lime (makrood) leaves.

14 oz	pork loin	400 g
1 lb	winter melon	500 g
1	can (19 oz/540 mL) coconut milk	1
2 tbsp	Kua Curry Paste (see page 108)	30 mL
4 tbsp	fish sauce	60 mL
5 tbsp	tamarind puree	75 mL
1 tbsp	fructose	15 mL
1 cup	water	250 mL
4	wild lime (makrood) leaves	4

Slice pork loin into medallions of about 1/3 inch (8 mm) thickness. Peel winter melon and cut into 1 1/2-2 inch (4-5 cm) chunks.

Spoon the solidified cream from coconut milk into a heavy saucepan or wok. Melt cream over medium heat, add Kua Curry Paste and fry gently 2 minutes.

Add coconut milk to curry paste and stir gently until mixture comes to the boil. Add pork loin and boil gently 5 minutes.

Add fish sauce, tamarind puree and fructose, mixing well. Add water (slosh it around in the coconut milk can to get the last of the coconut milk), winter melon and wild lime leaves. Bring to the boil, reduce heat and simmer gently 30 minutes. **Serves 4-6.**

TASTE

SWEET

PINEAPPLE SHRIMP CURRY
Gaeng Kua Sapparot

The flavours of this dish are incomparable. It's the play of the fresh pineapple against the strong curry, held together by coconut milk, that makes this curry so special. Be sure to use raw shrimp but feel free to choose any size you like.

1	can (19 oz/540 mL) coconut milk	1
2 tbsp	Kua Curry Paste (see page 108)	30 mL
1	pineapple	1
4	wild lime (makrood) leaves	4
	Fish sauce and fructose (optional)	
1 lb	shrimp, peeled and deveined	500 g
	Slivered chillies	
	Fresh Thai basil and coriander leaves	

Spoon the solidified cream from top of coconut milk into a heavy-bottomed pan or wok. Melt over medium heat; blend in Kua Curry Paste and continue to cook 5 minutes or until the mixture begins to darken and give off an aromatic, spicy smell.

Meanwhile, peel and core pineapple and chop into bite-sized pieces. Save any of the juice that runs off during the chopping process.

Tear wild lime leaves into several pieces and add to coconut mixture along with the pineapple and juice. Bring to the boil and cook 5 minutes. Taste and adjust the seasonings with fish sauce and fructose if necessary.

Add shrimp and boil rapidly for 5 minutes or until shrimp are pink but still tender. Garnish with chillies and basil and coriander leaves and serve immediately. **Serves 6**.

TASTE
SWEET
HOT

PANANG CURRY PASTE
Krung Gaeng Panang

If a milder curry paste is desired, remove seeds from chillies before pounding.

8	dried red chillies, or to taste	8
2	cloves garlic	2
2	shallots	2
1	stalk lemon grass	1
1 tbsp	grated wild lime (makrood) peel	15 mL
1 tbsp	chopped galanga (kha) root	15 mL
2	fresh coriander roots	2
1 tsp	coarsely ground black pepper	5 mL
1 tbsp	fish sauce	15 mL
1/2 tsp	fructose	2 mL
1 tbsp	finely chopped roasted peanuts	15 mL
1/2 tsp	shrimp paste (kapi)	2 mL

In a mortar and pounding in one at a time and mixing well after each addition, pound red chillies, then garlic, shallots, lemon grass, wild lime peel, galanga root, coriander roots, black pepper, fish sauce, fructose, peanuts and shrimp paste. **Makes 6 tbsp (90 mL), enough for two batches of curry.**

You may start the process in a food processor but to get the true flavours out of your ingredients you must end with 3-5 minutes of vigorous pounding by hand. When using a food processor, do not add peanuts and kapi until you reach the hand-pounding stage.

PANANG BEEF CURRY
Panang Nua

Our guests sometimes wonder why a Thai curry would be named after a Malaysian island. The simple answer is: it's not! Although the two words read alike when transliterated into English, the island is pronounced pee-nong; this thick curry pa-nang with a long "a" as in "gang."

Because it requires a long cooking time to make it nice and thick, this curry lends itself beautifully to the tougher cuts of beef. It tastes equally good with other meats, though.

1	can (19 oz/540 mL) coconut milk	1
14 oz	beef flank (or blade)	400 g
3 tbsp	Panang Curry Paste (see page 112)	45 mL
	Handful fresh chillies, if desired	
	Fish sauce, to taste	
	Fructose, to taste	
	Fresh coriander (or finely shredded lime leaves), for garnish	

In a heavy-bottomed pan, bring the coconut milk to the boil over medium-high heat. Slice beef fairly thinly and boil in the coconut milk 15 minutes, or until nearly tender. Remove beef and continue to boil milk 20 minutes until the oil begins to separate out.

Add curry paste, stir well, then return beef to the pan. If you like your curries extremely hot, add some fresh chillies as a vegetable at this point. Continue cooking 30 minutes over medium heat, or until the curry is thick. Adjust seasonings with fish sauce and fructose if necessary. Garnish with coriander or lime leaves. **Serves 4.**

TASTE
HOT
SALTY

ROASTED CHILLI PASTE
Nam Prik Pau

This simple paste is especially useful if you want to "spice up" a clear soup such as Lemon Shrimp Soup (see page 67), or a simple stir-fried dish.

3 tbsp	shrimp paste (kapi)	45 mL
6 tbsp	dried tamarind	90 mL
1/2 cup	boiling water	125 mL
6	shallots	6
6	large cloves garlic	6
6 tbsp	vegetable oil	90 mL
10	dried red chillies	10
4 tbsp	dried shrimp	60 mL
2 tbsp	fructose	30 mL

Stir-fry the shrimp paste in hot, dry wok or roast in the oven at high heat until dark brown.

Pour 1/2 cup (125 mL) boiling water over tamarind in a bowl and let it soak for 10 minutes. Work the tamarind and water together with your hands, and then sieve through a fairly fine-meshed strainer. Discard pulp and seeds.

Chop the shallots and garlic. Roast in a hot oven (400°F/200°C) on an oiled baking tray for 5 minutes.

Heat 2 tbsp (30 mL) oil in wok; fry chillies until crisp. Set aside. Fry the dried shrimp in the same oil until crisp.

In a bowl or mortar, pound the chillies, shrimp, shrimp paste, shallots, and garlic together to a smooth paste.

Heat 4 tbsp (60 mL) oil over medium heat in a heavy saucepan. Add the chilli mixture and stir. Stir in the fructose and tamarind liquid. Cook over medium heat for 30 minutes, stirring constantly, until mixture is smooth and the oil begins to separate. Can be stored many months, covered, in a cool place. **Makes about 1 cup (250 mL).**

PHOTO: *Pineapple Shrimp Curry (page 111) shown with (from left) lemon grass, pineapple, wild lime, coconut, shallot, dried chillies, krachai root (resting on pestle) and coriander root*

OVERLEAF PHOTO: *Fish deep-fried Thai style should be extremely crispy: Neptune's Nemesis (page 126) shown with and without sauce, together with dried tamarind and fresh finger chilli*

CHAPTER 8
FISH AND SHELLFISH

"We have fish in the waters and rice in the fields" is a Thai adage that has survived from the 13th century. Even in times of extreme poverty, Thais believe the lands and the waters yield enough food for even the destitute to survive.

Along many thousands of miles of seacoast on both the Gulf of Siam and the Andaman Sea, fleets of fishing vessels set out from hundreds of fishing villages to harvest a rich crop of fish, squid, crab, shrimp, mussels and lobsters from the teeming tropical waters.

Fresh seafood makes its way to city markets: at Bangrak, the main wholesale fish market for Bangkok, baskets heaped with fish still wriggling on their beds of ice and shrimps of every size threatening to jump out of their baskets are brought ashore before dawn. Most of the fish eaten in Bangkok and other towns and cities near the sea is fresh-caught that day.

What can't be eaten that day is dried in the brilliant tropical sun. Shrimp, squids of many sizes, firm-fleshed fish and tiny sprat-like fish are dried in a matter of days, then shipped inland for consumption by the farmers in the central and northern agricultural districts.

Other fish are processed into the salty fish sauce that gives that special "Thai" flavour to Thai food. The fish is cleaned and placed in earthenware crocks, layers of fish alternating with layers of salt until the crock is full. The crocks are sealed and left in the sun while the salt draws the flavours from the fish. When the fish sauce has matured, it is drawn from the crocks, filtered and bottled. Fish sauce is a staple in every Thai kitchen, and is used instead of salt in most dishes.

Fresh shellfish was the inspiration for the fiery Sriracha sauce, the bright red one we serve in Bangkok Garden. Made of hot chilli peppers, salt, vinegar and a dash of sugar, it was invented in the Thai fishing port of Sriracha as a condiment for the fresh shrimp caught by the Sriracha fishing fleet. Two large factories now manufacture and bottle this hot Thai sauce to tickle the palates of a chilli-loving nation. It would be unthinkable to serve shellfish in Thailand without offering a bottle of Sriracha sauce.

Inland, freshwater fish are harvested from rivers, ponds and rice paddies. Catfish is a particularly popular freshwater fish and appears in regional curries, soups and condiments.

At Bangkok Garden, we've experimented with both fresh- and saltwater fish and have found that they perform equally well in curries, soups and whole fish presentations such as Steamed Ginger Fish (see page 130) and Pla Laad Prik (see page 126).

Our experience also tells us that we don't have to stick slavishly to fish that would normally be found in the Gulf of Siam. North American waters yield a rich harvest of fish and shellfish that marry well with Thai flavours and cooking methods.

LIME AND GINGER SQUID
Yum Pla Muk

These are the tenderest squid you've ever tasted! Light, refreshing and extremely low in calories, this is a favourite lunch dish at Bangkok Garden. Serve it with sticky rice, raw vegetables and a clear soup for lunch, or as the hot and sour dish in a selection of dinner entrées.

10	stalks fresh mint	10
1	coriander plant (6-10 stalks)	1
3	shallots	3
2	hot red (or green) chillies, or to taste	2
1	green onion	1
1 lb	baby squid	500 g
3 tbsp	lime juice	45 mL
2 tbsp	fish sauce	30 mL
1/2 tsp	fructose	2 mL
1 tbsp	finely julienned ginger root	15 mL
1 tbsp	roasted rice powder (see page 23)	15 mL

Garnish

Lettuce leaves
Cucumber
Grated carrots
Tomato wedges
Lime wedges
Fresh chilli peppers

Remove leaves from mint and coriander and keep whole. Discard the stalks. Freeze the coriander root for later use in a curry paste. Slice shallots, chillies and green onion and combine with leaves.

Wash squid thoroughly; remove tentacle portions. (Only the white bodies are used in this dish. You can use the tentacles in a seafood soup or a stir-fried rice dish.) Score the white flesh 5 or 6 times with a sharp knife.

Cook squid by steaming or plunging into rapidly boiling water for 3 minutes or just until squid curls up. Drain thoroughly, then toss with lime juice, fish sauce, fructose, ginger, mint and coriander mixture and roasted rice powder.

Garnish to taste and serve immediately. **Serves 2-4.**

The lime juice will cause the vegetables to wilt and the squid to go mushy; do not prepare more than 15 minutes before serving.

For a hotter dish, bruise chillies before slicing— this releases the volatile oil capsaicin, which gives the chillies their bite.

TASTE

HOT
SOUR

MUSSELS "BANGRAK"
Hoy Tot

Not quite an omelette and not quite a crepe, this versatile dish could be anything from a dinner course to a luncheon dish to the market breakfast it really is.

This dish originates in Bangrak Market, Bangkok's main seafood wholesale market, on New Street just a few blocks from the venerable Oriental Hotel. Fishing vessels pull up to Bangrak's bustling docks all night, disgorging their baskets of freshly caught fish and shellfish from the Gulf of Siam.

Here at Bangrak, restaurateurs and hotel chefs select their fresh seafood, still wriggling and jumping in straw baskets. When the marketing is over, usually well before the sun rises, shoppers settle down to a hearty breakfast of seafood crepe/omelette before returning to their kitchens to begin the day's preparations for Bangkok's legions of hungry diners.

Crepe Batter		
5 tbsp	rice flour	75 mL
1 tbsp	sticky rice flour	15 mL
2-3 tbsp	cold water	30-50 mL
1 tbsp	finely sliced green onion	15 mL

Omelette Mixture		
2 tsp	vegetable oil	10 mL
10	fresh mussels, shelled	10
2	eggs	2
	Handful bean sprouts, or to taste	
1 tbsp	finely chopped green onion	15 mL
1 tbsp	fresh coriander leaves	15 mL
1 tsp	fish sauce	5 mL
1 tsp	Crispy Fried Garlic in Oil (see page 66)	5 mL
Pinch	pepper, or to taste	Pinch
Pinch	fructose, or to taste	Pinch

Put rice flour and sticky rice flour in a small bowl. Slowly add water, stirring vigorously, until batter is the consistency of table cream, adding more water if necessary to achieve proper consistency. Add green onion and stir. The mixture will settle, so stir well before cooking.

Heat a griddle or omelette pan until a drop of water sizzles on the surface. Add 1-2 tsp (5-10 mL) oil and heat. Pour about

T
A
S
T
E

SWEET
SALTY

3 tbsp (45 mL) of batter onto pan and wait until it has spread. Sprinkle mussels on top and cook 3 minutes.

Break eggs and pour over the mussel mixture. Muddle eggs with a chopstick or fork. Sprinkle with bean sprouts, green onion, coriander leaves, fish sauce, crispy fried garlic, pepper and fructose; cook until egg is set. Fold, remove from griddle, cut into pieces and serve with your favourite dipping sauce.

Serves 2-4, depending on the number of other dishes offered—or it can be a whole meal for one.

GARLIC PEPPER SHRIMP
Kung Tod Grathiem Prik Tai

To my mind, this dish is at its best when you use lots of pepper, and large shrimp with the tails on.

If you don't have coriander roots, use fresh coriander stems. This will give a greenish cast to the dish, but the taste is still great!

10	fresh coriander roots	10
1 tsp	salt	5 mL
1 tsp	pepper	5 mL
10	cloves garlic	10
1 lb	shrimp (any size), peeled and deveined	500 g
5 tbsp	vegetable oil	75 mL

Pound coriander roots, salt, pepper and garlic together in a mortar. Toss shrimp in this mixture.

Heat oil in a wok until it smokes. Add shrimp and stir-fry over very high heat until shrimp are pink and opaque.

If you are using frozen shrimp, you may get a watery gravy. In that case, lift shrimp out to a serving platter and reduce pan gravy by continuing to cook over high heat, stirring constantly, until most of the water has evaporated. Pour the remaining sauce over the shrimp. **Serves 4.**

If you like the bite and flavour of black pepper, increase amount accordingly. I like at least 1 tbsp (15 mL).

SALTY

QUENELLES OF WHITE FISH & QUENELLES OF SHRIMP
Luuk Cheen

Traditional Thai fish quenelles (or "fish balls") are very mildly seasoned as they are often served in a delicate broth. They may also be served in a fiery-hot curry sauce laced with shredded lime leaves, ginger and whole chillies. They may be round or oval in shape, about half the size of a ping-pong ball.

Most Oriental markets carry them in their frozen food section where the quenelles are traditionally round or flat as if sliced from a French baguette-shaped loaf. Store-bought quenelles tend to contain MSG, sugar and a lot of flour.

The beauty of making your own is that you can use any kind of fish—fresh or salt, white, pink or yellow-fleshed. And the taste is fresher, lighter, better.

QUENELLES OF WHITE FISH

1 lb	fresh white fish fillets: cod, sole, sea bass, etc.	500 g
1 tbsp	cornstarch (or tapioca or sticky rice flour)	15 mL
1/2 tsp	salt	2 mL
1/2 tsp	white pepper	2 mL
1/2 tsp	fructose (or honey or other sweetener), if desired	2 mL

Lay raw fish fillets on a flat surface and scrape with an inverted spoon. Discard sinews. In a mortar, pound fish well, about 5 minutes, until a smooth, sticky paste. Add cornstarch, salt, pepper and fructose, if desired, and mix well. Form into small balls and poach 5 minutes in rapidly boiling water. Drain.

Use quenelles the same day, or freeze for later use. **Makes 40-50 quenelles.**

QUENELLES OF SHRIMP

1 lb	small shrimp, peeled and deveined	500 g
1/4 tsp	salt	1 mL
1/2 tsp	white pepper	2 mL
1 tsp	lime juice	5 mL
1/2 tsp	fructose (or honey or other sweetener)	2 mL
1/4 tsp	red paprika (for colour, as desired)	1 mL

TASTE
SWEET
SALTY

Sprinkle shrimp with salt, pepper, lime juice and fructose. Pound to a paste in a mortar until smooth and sticky. Add red paprika, if desired. Mix well. Form into small balls and poach 5 minutes in boiling water. Drain. Use quenelles the same day, or freeze for later use. Makes 40-50 quenelles (1 lb/500 g).

BBQ FISH KEBABS
Luuk Cheen Ping

This is a favourite snack for motorists who purchase these kebabs from children who move nimbly among the cars at rush hour.

You can make your quenelles small, thread them on short skewers and serve as appetisers, or make them larger and serve them as a main course dish with perhaps a noodle, a stir-fried vegetable and a salad dish.

In Thailand, the quenelles are threaded on the skewers by themselves and served with dipping sauce and a side dish of lightly steamed vegetables.

40-50	Quenelles of White Fish (see page opposite)	40-50
40-50	Quenelles of Shrimp (see page opposite)	40-50
20	6-inch/15 cm (or 10-inch/25 cm) bamboo skewers	20
30	small red and green chillies and/or 30 firm cherry tomatoes Vegetable oil for brushing	30

Thread fish and shrimp quenelles onto skewers with chillies and/or tomatoes. Brush with oil and barbecue 5 to 10 minutes.

Serve with your favourite dipping sauce (see pages 62-63) or Sriracha straight from the bottle. **Makes approximately 20 skewers.** Most people will eat 1 or 2 as an appetiser; 3 as a main course with other dishes.

To prevent bamboo skewers from burning, soak in water for a few hours before using.

TASTE
SWEET

VEGETABLE SEAFOOD CURRY
Gaeng Luuk Cheen Pla

A good Thai curry should have a generous layer of coconut oil shimmering on top. Do not skim this.

This is one of Thailand's favourite curries—and very easy to make if you purchase the curry paste and fish quenelles at the supermarket. Don't hesitate to put your own personal stamp on this curry by adding other vegetables as desired.

3/4 cup	coconut cream	175 mL
5 tbsp	Green Curry Paste (see page 101)	75 mL
1	can (19 oz/540 mL) bamboo shoots, drained and julienned	1
5 cups	coconut milk	1.25 L
8-10	wild lime (makrood) leaves, torn roughly	8-10
2 tbsp	fish sauce	30 mL
40-50	fish quenelles (see page 120)	40-50
1 cup	baby Thai eggplant (or 2 cups/500 mL cubed regular eggplant)	250 mL

Garnish

3	chillies, slivered	3
1	stalk fresh Thai basil (10-20 leaves)	1
2-3	stalks fresh coriander leaves (optional)	2-3

In a wok or a very heavy-bottomed pan, cook coconut cream, stirring, over medium heat until the liquid is reduced somewhat and the coconut oil begins to separate and rise to the surface.

Add the Green Curry Paste, increase heat slightly, and continue cooking for approximately 5 minutes or until the mixture begins to darken and give off a strong "cooked" smell. When curry begins to bubble, reduce heat to low, cover and continue cooking 15 minutes, stirring occasionally.

Meanwhile, soak bamboo shoots in cold water or boil hard in water for 10 minutes to draw out some of the brine. Drain.

Add coconut milk, wild lime leaves and fish sauce to curry mixture and bring to a boil. Reduce heat to simmer and continue cooking, uncovered, about 10 minutes. Add fish quenelles, eggplant and bamboo shoots; cook for 10 minutes.

To serve, sprinkle curry with chillies and basil and coriander leaves. Serve with plain steamed rice. **Serves 4-6.**

TASTE

SWEET
SALTY
HOT

STIR-FRIED SCALLOPS WITH GARLIC AND BASIL
Hoy Shell Phad Baay Krapao

This is a very rich dish and one that works well with European broad-leaved basil. You might want to consider adding some vegetables to this dish.

Scallops come in a range of sizes, from small marble-sized ones all the way to sweet Pacific ones nearly the size of golf balls. If you are using the very small ones, chop or tear the basil leaves slightly before adding them to the stir-fry. At Bangkok Garden we occasionally slice the large scallops into rounds and mix in water chestnuts cut the same way. The pieces look similar but there's an intense difference between the crunchy water chestnut and the soft sweet flesh of the scallop—an endearing Thai culinary pun you might enjoy playing with.

4	cloves garlic	4
10	stalks fresh Thai basil	10
	(about 1/2 cup/125 mL leaves)	
2 tbsp	vegetable oil	30 mL
1 lb	scallops	500 g
1 tbsp	fermented soya beans (optional)	15 mL
1 tbsp	fish sauce	15 mL
1 tsp	ground pepper	5 mL

Smash garlic, then chop. Remove basil leaves from stalks, wash and dry.

In a wok or heavy frying pan, heat oil until it smokes. Add garlic, stir a few times. Add scallops; stir-fry 2-5 minutes or until white and firm.

Add basil leaves, fermented soya beans (if desired), fish sauce and pepper; stir gently 2 minutes until mixture returns to the boil and basil leaves are wilted.

Serve immediately. Serves 4-6.

For a hotter dish, add a handful of sliced fresh chillies along with the garlic, or stir a tablespoonful (15 mL) of fresh chilli paste in with the fermented soya beans.

TASTE
SALTY
SWEET

SWEET AND SOUR BREADED FISH
Pla Priau Waan

Thai sweet and sour is quite different from that of other nationalities. The sweetness and acidity come from the fruit and vegetables themselves, with sugar or lime juice added only if an imbalance is detected at the end of the cooking process. The other ingredient that makes Thai sweet and sour stand out is the cucumber. In Thailand, small oval-shaped cucumbers are widely used. In pickling season, you can use small gherkin cucumbers. At other times of the year, English cucumbers are best as they stand up well to cooking. Any cucumber will do, however.

1 lb	firm-fleshed fish such as cod, haddock, snapper or grouper	500 g
2 cups	vegetable oil for deep-frying	500 mL
6	stalks fresh coriander	6

Sweet and sour sauce

1	medium ripe pineapple	1
8	Roma tomatoes, quartered (or 16 cherry tomatoes, halved)	8
2	small cooking onions	2
4	green onions	4
1	sweet red pepper (optional)	1
2 or 3	tender small celery stalks, with leaves	2 or 3
1	English cucumber	1
4	cloves garlic	4
2 tbsp	light vegetable oil	30 mL
1	large carrot, cut in thin rounds	1
1 tbsp	fish sauce	15 mL
1 tsp	ground pepper	5 mL

Batter

1	egg	1
1 tbsp	light vegetable oil	15 mL
1/2 cup	sticky rice flour	125 mL
1/2 cup	cornstarch (or tapioca flour)	125 mL
1/2 tsp	baking powder	2 mL
1 tsp	salt	5 mL
	Water	

TASTE

SWEET
SOUR

Sweet and sour sauce: Peel pineapple and chop fairly fine, making sure you keep all the juices. Cut tomatoes and reserve the juice. Cut cooking onions in wedges, then cut each wedge in half so you end up with large slightly curved triangles. Slice green onions in half lengthwise, then cut into 1 1/2-inch (4 cm) lengths. Cut red pepper into triangles, if using. Chop celery stalks coarsely. Cut cucumber into thick triangular wedges by cutting in half lengthwise, then cutting lengthwise again into quarters or sixths. Then cut into 2-inch (6 cm) lengths. Bruise garlic, then chop.

Heat oil in a wok until it begins to swirl around and run thin but not until it smokes. Add chopped garlic, stir a few times. Add green onions, cooking onions, carrot, cucumber, celery and red pepper; stir-fry 3-4 minutes, until onions start to go transparent. Add tomatoes and pineapple with juices. Bring to the boil, reduce heat and simmer 5 minutes. Remove from heat, stir in fish sauce and pepper. Set aside.

Batter: Beat egg well, add oil and beat until well mixed. In bowl, combine rice flour, cornstarch, baking powder and salt. Stir in egg mixture, blending well to a smooth cream. Add water until the batter is the consistency of yogurt and runs smoothly off the spoon.

To prepare fish, pat dry and cut into bite-sized chunks.

Heat oil in a wok or deep-fryer until it starts to smoke. Dip fish pieces in batter and deep-fry about 8 pieces at a time, until batter is crisp and golden brown. Remove to a paper towel and continue frying until all fish is cooked. Set aside and keep warm.

To finish, heat sauce through. Add fish, stir to mix. Spoon onto a platter, garnish with coriander and serve immediately. Serves 4-6.

The pineapple itself is sweet and sour, the tomatoes are sour and the onions, carrots and sweet pepper are sweet. You can adjust the sweetness and acidity further with the addition of fructose and lime juice or vinegar. This sauce will be very runny: if you like it thicker you can thicken it before adding the deep-fried fish by adding 1 tbsp (15 mL) cornstarch moistened with water or soup stock and stirring until clear and thickened.

To make the sauce hotter, bruise the garlic and the chillies with the flat of a knife blade before chopping.

Remember that the longer you cook the chillies, the hotter the sauce will be!

NEPTUNE'S NEMESIS
Pla Laad Prik

The great joy of this dish is the contrast of the crispy crunch of the fried fish with the sweet-hot smoothness of the sauce.

For the calorie-conscious, we have made this dish with thick chunks of steamed fish and also, interestingly, with grilled boneless chicken breast.

The traditional Thai method, a whole fish crisp-fried and smothered with sauce, is by far the most dramatic presentation.

2-3 cups	vegetable oil for deep-frying	500-750 mL
14 oz	fillet of fish (or 1 lb/500 g whole fish)	400 g
1	green onion, chopped	1
6	stalks fresh coriander	6
12	slices cucumber	12
	Sauce	
1 cup	light vegetable oil	250 mL
4 tbsp	chopped garlic	60 mL
2/3 cup	chopped shallots	150 mL
2/3 cup	chopped fresh chillies	150 mL
2 cups	tamarind puree	500 mL
1 tbsp	fructose	15 mL
1 tbsp	fish sauce	15 mL

Sauce: Heat 1 cup (250 mL) light vegetable oil in a saucepan over medium heat to just below the smoking point.

Add the chopped garlic to the hot oil all at once. The oil will foam up dramatically with a great hissing. As soon as the bubbles die down, give the garlic a stir. It will be properly cooked by then.

Stir in the chopped shallots and chillies. Cook 5 minutes on medium heat, stirring occasionally, until chillies and shallots have softened. Add the tamarind puree, fructose and fish sauce. Stir until blended. Lower the heat and simmer, stirring occasionally, until the sauce is thick, 10-15 minutes.

While the sauce is cooking, heat the oil for deep-frying in a wok until it is very hot. Make several deep diagonal cuts on each side of the fish. Place the fish in the hot oil (it will foam and sputter) and immediately lower the heat to medium so that the

TASTE

HOT
SWEET

fish does not burn. Continue frying until the outside of the fish becomes very crispy, approximately 10 minutes. For fish fillets, omit the diagonal cuts and reduce cooking time to 5 minutes, or whatever the thickness of the fillet demands. The flesh should be crisp right through.

Remove the fish to a platter and pour the sauce over top. Garnish with chopped green onions and fresh coriander. Serve with sliced cucumber for decoration as well as for its cooling effect. **Serves 2-4.**

SEA BASS STIR-FRIED WITH CURRY POWDER
Pla Phad Pong Garee

Here's a simple dish you can prepare with any firm-fleshed fish. Be sure not to cook it too long.

14 oz	sea bass steak (or fillet)	400 g
3 tbsp	vegetable oil	45 mL
4 tsp	Madras curry powder	20 mL
1/2 cup	water	125 mL
3 tbsp	fish sauce	45 mL
2 1/2 tbsp	fructose	38 mL
1	cooking onion, cut in thin wedges	1
Half	sweet red pepper, slivered	Half

Wash and dry sea bass (if necessary) and cut into 1/2-inch (1 cm) slices.

Heat oil in a wok. Add curry powder and fry, stirring constantly, about 2 minutes. Add water and boil gently over medium heat 5 minutes.

Add fish, mix well and stir-fry 3 minutes. Add fish sauce, fructose and onion, bring to the boil and cook 2 minutes.

Turn onto a platter, sprinkle with red pepper and serve immediately. **Serves 2-4.**

TASTE
SALTY

STEAMED FISH WITH COCONUT
Hormok

Hormok is one of those Thai curiosities that defies description. It appears as an appetiser in Curried Mussels on the Half Shell (see page 58).

It tastes like a curry but it's set like a custard. You can steam it in fish-shaped containers, small bowls, jelly molds or any shape that takes your fancy.

Thais love this dish powerfully hot, but you can adjust the "heat" by using black pepper and chilli peppers to your taste.

If fresh Thai basil leaves are not available, substitute cabbage or spinach leaves.

14 oz	fish fillets	400 g
3 tbsp	Red Curry Paste (see page 104)	45 mL
2 tbsp	fish sauce	30 mL
2 oz	unsweetened shredded coconut	50 g
	Salt and freshly ground black pepper	
2	eggs	2
1/2 cup	cooked whole cabbage leaves	125 mL
1	fresh red chilli pepper	1
1	fresh green chilli pepper	1
1 cup	fresh Thai basil leaves	250 mL
1 cup	coconut cream	250 mL
3	wild lime (makrood) leaves, very finely shredded	3
10	stalks fresh coriander, for garnish	10
	Thai basil leaves, to taste, for garnish	
	Other garnish as desired	

Flake the fish and place into a large bowl. Add the curry paste, fish sauce and shredded coconut and stir to blend. Season to taste with salt and freshly ground pepper. Add eggs and stir until thoroughly blended. The mixture should be thick and creamy; if it is too stiff (say, as stiff as a pastry dough), add a small quantity of coconut cream.

Shred the cabbage and cut the red and green chillies into fine julienne strips. Line a 3-cup (750 mL) mold or pan with the basil leaves and layer shredded cabbage over top. Add the fish mixture and top with coconut cream, strips of chilli and shredded wild lime leaves. Cover the pan, place over boiling water and steam for 25-30 minutes, until the mixture has set.

To serve, unmold onto a serving platter and garnish with coriander leaves, Thai basil leaves, carved vegetables or whatever is seasonally available. **Serves 2-4.**

TASTE
HOT
SALTY

STEAMED FISH WITH LIME SAUCE
Pla Nung Menau

You can make this incredibly easy dish with a wide variety of freshwater and saltwater fish.

Try trout, young salmon, snapper, bass, perch, sole or other flatfish.

1	whole fish, about 2 lb/1 kg	1
10-15	fresh chillies	10-15
4	cloves garlic	4
3 tbsp	fish sauce	45 mL
4 tbsp	lime juice	60 mL
1/2 tsp	fructose	2 mL

Garnish
Half	sweet red pepper, slivered	Half
2	green onions, cut in 2 1/2-inch/ 6 cm lengths and slivered	2
6	stalks fresh coriander	6

Wash and clean fish. Trim off fins with scissors but otherwise leave whole. Make 3 diagonal cuts through the body.

Steam in a stovetop steamer about 15 minutes (according to size and thickness of fish) until flesh is opaque. A flatfish such as sole or flounder may take about 10 minutes; a thicker fish such as salmon may take 15 minutes. You can do this in a microwave; adjust cooking time accordingly.

Meanwhile, chop chillies and garlic very fine. Add fish sauce, lime juice and fructose and mix well. Taste and adjust seasoning.

Put fish on serving platter, pour sauce over, garnish with red pepper, green onions and coriander. **Serves 4.**

For best colour effect, use both green and red chillies.

TASTE

SOUR
HOT

STEAMED GINGER FISH
Pla Nung

The indescribable flavour of the krachai root is impossible to mistake—and impossible to duplicate if you cannot find fresh or frozen krachai root.

Do not panic. Although it will be a different dish, this delicate steamed fish will taste just as delightful if you use a thumb-sized piece of ginger, sliced lengthwise into 6-8 pieces.

5	dried Chinese mushrooms	5
10	dried Chinese plums	10
1	whole fish (approx 2 lb/1 kg) (sea bass, pomfret or catfish) Salt	1
1	krachai root	1
10	fresh coriander stalks	10
3	green onions, cut in 2-inch/5 cm lengths	3
	Piece (4 inch/10 cm) ginger root, peeled and sliced very fine in shreds	
	Juice of 1 lime	

Garnish

Slivers of red chilli
Fresh coriander leaves

Wash dried mushrooms to remove sand and debris. Put mushrooms and plums in a small bowl and pour over boiling water to cover. Allow to soak 30 minutes, or until mushrooms are soft. Reserve a few tablespoons soaking water. Slice mushrooms in julienne.

Clean and scale the fish and wash thoroughly. Trim any ragged edges on fins and tail. Wipe out the cavity and sprinkle a little salt inside. Wash and bruise krachai root and put inside the cavity with the coriander stalks.

Steam the fish in the serving dish you plan to use on the table by placing the fish in the serving dish; sprinkle julienned mushrooms, soaked plums, green onions and shredded ginger over the fish. Pour the reserved soaking water and the lime juice over the fish. Steam in a Chinese-style stovetop steamer with the water boiling hard underneath for about 20 minutes.

Before serving, discard coriander stalks and krachai root. Garnish with slivers of red chilli and fresh coriander leaves. If desired, serve this dish with a hot chilli sauce. **Serves 2-4.**

TASTE
SLIGHTLY
SWEET
SLIGHTLY
HOT

TOTSAKAN'S REVENGE
Pla Chu Chee

This mild, lemony curry is quite runny and can be made with almost any kind of freshwater or saltwater fish. We have found any type that can be cut into steaks will do well here.

Try salmon, trout, halibut, cod, mahi-mahi, sea bass or tilapia.

2	cans (each 14 oz/398 mL) coconut milk	2
1 tbsp	Red Curry Paste (see page 104)	15 mL
4-5	wild lime (makrood) leaves	4-5
1 tbsp	fructose	15 mL
2 tbsp	fish sauce	30 mL
2 lb	fish steaks or fillets, preferably boneless	1 kg

Fresh Thai basil leaves, for garnish

Remove any cream from coconut milk to a wok. If there is no cream, put 2-3 tbsp (30-45 mL) light vegetable oil in wok. Heat over high heat and fry curry paste about 5 minutes, or until fragrant.

Gradually stir in remaining coconut milk, bring to the boil, reduce heat slightly and boil gently 20 minutes.

Meanwhile, shred the wild lime leaves very finely. Add to the curry sauce along with the fructose and fish sauce. Taste for seasoning and add more fish sauce or fructose if desired.

Add the fish to the curry sauce. Boil gently 10 minutes or until opaque, but not falling apart.

Serve in a bowl, garnished with fresh basil leaves. **Serves 4.**

TASTE
SALTY

STIR-FRIED CLAMS IN THE SHELL
Hoy Shell Phad

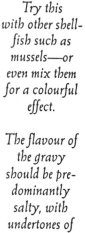

*Try this
with other shell-
fish such as
mussels—or
even mix them
for a colourful
effect.*

*The flavour of
the gravy
should be pre-
dominantly
salty, with
undertones of
sour.*

I was astonished to learn, on a trip to a Thai seaside fishing village, that shellfish dishes like this one are created using exactly the same method as you would for chicken or rice or vegetables.

Once you get used to the idea of stir-frying something that clicks and clacks around the pan, it makes perfectly good sense.

2 lb	clams	1 kg
4	cloves garlic	4
1	sweet red pepper	1
1	coriander plant, including root	1
1 tsp	black peppercorns	5 mL
4 tbsp	vegetable oil	60 mL
2 tbsp	fish sauce	30 mL
2 tsp	fructose	10 mL
2 tsp	shrimp paste (kapi)	10 mL
2 tbsp	fermented soya beans	30 mL
	Leaves from large stalk Thai basil	1
	Juice of 2 limes	
2	green onions	2
	Slivered chillies for garnish	

Soak clams in cold water and scrub well. Discard any that do not close.

Smash garlic with the flat of a knife blade and chop. Slice red pepper in thin strips.

Remove coriander leaves and reserve for garnish. Chop the stems and roots roughly and pound to a pulp. Add peppercorns and pound to a rough paste.

Heat oil in a large, heavy-bottomed wok over high heat until it smokes. Add garlic and deep-fry until brown. Add pounded coriander-pepper paste and clams and stir well until clams are all coated with oil. Continue stirring about 3 minutes. Add a little water, cover immediately and let steam 1 minute.

Add red pepper, fish sauce, fructose, shrimp paste, fermented soya beans and basil leaves. Stir well, cover and let cook 2 minutes.

Add lime juice. Discard any clams that have not opened. Taste the gravy and adjust the seasonings.

Mound on a serving platter or bowl and garnish with chopped green onions, coriander leaves and chillies. Make sure to spoon the pan gravy over your rice! **Serves 2-4.**

TASTE
SALTY

CHAPTER 9
MEAT AND POULTRY

Although it appears in almost every dish, meat is not a central focus in Thai cuisine. Rice, fish, vegetables and salt in the form of fish sauce form the basis of the Thai diet, today and historically.

King Ramkamhaeng (1275-1317), the great agriculturalist king of the Sukhothai (AD 1238-1340) era, gave his attention to the growing of fruit and vegetable crops, and the raising of fish in ponds. For special occasions, the men hunted game such as wild boar and venison. But hunting has never been popular in Thailand and, due to a Buddhist edict against killing, hunting and fishing are not allowed on the numerous Buddhist holy days. Fruit, rice and fish were the foods of the common people. Meat or game appeared only infrequently—and only in the royal or aristocratic kitchens.

When King Ramathibodhi founded the Ayuthaya empire in 1350, he planted his kingdom squarely in the middle of two powerful cultural influences: the Buddhist Mon to the west and the Brahmin Khmer to the east. The Siamese eventually conquered the Khmer empire, sacked the capital and in AD 1440 carried the entire Royal Court back to Ayuthaya—cooks, artists, religious advisors and all. In the resulting melting-pot of customs and cultures, it is likely the Thai were influenced by both Buddhist and Brahmin proscriptions against killing.

A 16th-century French visitor reported that the Thai diet consisted largely of rice with fish and vegetables, and that although they had ducks and two kinds of chickens, they took little care for their poultry and ate it rarely.

Meat and poultry, then, tended to be served at celebrations, festivals and formal occasions. Even today with the vastly improved animal husbandry of the 20th century, few Thai dishes concentrate on meat as the focal ingredient.

In this book, meat quantities have been increased to reflect North American appetites.

No Thai cookbook would be complete without a barbecue recipe; I'm pleased to share a couple of Bangkok Garden favourites with you. Here you'll find the classic Laab Issan, both in the traditional beef version and in our chicken variation. You'll be happy to hear it's easy to find all the ingredients necessary for this classic.

*To make
this dish hotter,
add 1 or more
teaspoons
(5 mL)
of Roasted
Chilli Paste
(see page 114)
along with the
garlic-
coriander
paste.*

TOASTED CASHEWS WITH CHICKEN
Gai Phad Met Mamuang

We knew long before we opened our doors that this was a winner because during the two years of trial runs it was the dish the staff most often requested—and it has remained a "must" for birthdays and other celebrations.

Don't cheat by using roasted, salted cashews for this dish. The flavour of the freshly toasted cashew is imperative to achieve the delicate balance of flavours in this deceptively simple dish.

It's important not to leave the cashews in the chicken mixture too long or they'll lose the crispness that is a hallmark of the dish. If you want to ensure that the dish remains mild, use only whole unbroken toasted chillies as garnish. Once the seeds spill out into the dish, it will start to "heat" up.

An added bonus of this dish is that it appeals to lovers of hot and mild alike, for it's only hot if you eat the toasted chilli garnish.

1 cup	raw cashew nuts	250 mL
16	dried red finger-hot chillies	16
2 oz	cloud ear mushrooms	50 g
	(or straw mushrooms) (optional)	
14 oz	boneless chicken breast	400 g
2	medium onions	2
2	green onions	2
2	cloves garlic	2
2	coriander roots	2
4 tbsp	vegetable oil	60 mL
2 tbsp	fish sauce	30 mL
1 tsp	fructose	5 mL
1 tsp	ground black pepper	5 mL
	Fresh coriander leaves for garnish	

Toast the cashews by stir-frying in a dry wok over high heat, stirring constantly to prevent burning. Set aside.

Now stand well back and prepare to cough a bit as you give the dried chillies the same treatment. The skins will turn from red to near-black and as they toast, the volatile oil of capsaicin will be released into the air. Try to imagine what this looks and smells like in the Bangkok Garden kitchen when the cooks toast the day's supply—some hundreds of chillies jumping and smoking

T
A
S
T
E
SWEET
SALTY
HOT
(IF DESIRED)

in the pan, and everyone in the area coughing and crying good-naturedly!

Soak cloud ear mushrooms in water 30 minutes. Rinse to remove all sand.

Slice chicken breast into bite-sized pieces. Cut onions into thin wedges. Cut green onions into 2-inch (5 cm) lengths, then halve or quarter lengthwise.

Pound garlic and coriander roots together to a paste.

Heat oil in a wok over high heat until it begins to smoke. Add garlic-coriander paste and stir-fry briefly, about 15 seconds. Add chicken and stir-fry until chicken is no longer pink, about 3 minutes. Push the chicken up the sides of the pan, add onion wedges and cook until they are limp and translucent, about 3 minutes. Add green onions and mushrooms; cook 1 minute. Stir everything in the pan together and season with fish sauce, fructose and pepper.

Keep everything boiling vigorously as you adjust the seasonings. Add toasted cashews, stir just enough to mix well. Serve immediately, garnished with toasted chillies and fresh coriander leaves. **Serves 4.**

Garlic, in combination with black pepper and fish sauce, is the building block for creating dishes that taste truly "Thai."
To create a quick and classic Thai barbecue marinade, pound garlic cloves in a mortar with whole black peppercorns (about half the quantity of the garlic), some fish sauce and fresh coriander roots. Spread this thick paste on chicken or beef pieces, let stand a while to allow the flavours to penetrate, then barbecue as usual.
You can use this same paste to stir-fry meats and vegetables. It gives them a wonderful curry-like flavour.

In this dish the basil is treated as a vegetable like spinach.

LIVER NARAI
Tap Gai Phad Baay Krapao

Even those who don't care much for liver tell us how much they enjoy this dish, which depends on the impact of fresh Thai basil leaves.

Cook this dish hot or mild according to the tastes of your guests. When I make this dish at home with basil leaves picked fresh from the garden, I use three or four different kinds of hot chillies for the hot version, and cook a separate pan without chillies for those who prefer to eat mild. Remarkably, it works both ways!

This dish requires an intense heat for the flavours to come out just right. These instructions have been written specifically for use with a domestic electric burner. If your burner delivers a higher heat, you may not have to remove the chicken livers while you cook the vegetables.

14 oz	chicken livers	400 g
2	cloves garlic	2
4	red finger-hot chillies, or to taste	4
1-2 cups	loosely packed fresh Thai basil leaves	250-500 mL
2	medium onions	2
4 tbsp	vegetable oil	60 mL
3 tbsp	fish sauce	45 mL
2 tsp	fructose	10 mL
1 tsp	ground pepper	5 mL
	Fresh basil leaves, for garnish	
	Chillies cut into flowers, for garnish	

Remove any stringy sinews from livers and cut into large chunks. Smash garlic cloves and chop. Slice chillies lengthwise, removing seeds for a milder dish. Wash basil leaves and remove fibrous stems. Cut onions in thin wedges.

In a wok, heat 2 tbsp (30 mL) of the oil over high heat until smoking. Add garlic, stir briefly. Add chicken livers and stir-fry over high heat until meat is seared and (if possible) crispy on the outside, about 3 minutes.

Remove chicken livers with a slotted spoon and set aside, keeping hot. Add remaining oil and heat until smoking. Add onions and chillies and stir-fry until onions are soft. Add basil leaves; stir-fry until basil leaves are wilted, about 1 minute.

Push vegetables up the sides of the pan, return chicken livers to the pan and sprinkle with fish sauce, fructose and black

T
A
S
T
E
BITTER

pepper. Cover and cook 1-2 minutes or until livers are hot. Stir all ingredients together, then push up the sides of the pan again. There should be a little gravy at the bottom of the pan. If necessary, add a splash of water and taste. Adjust the seasonings as the gravy boils down a bit.

Serve garnished with fresh basil leaves and chillies cut into flowers. **Serves 4.**

KIDS' CURRY
Khaay Pulao

This dish, predominantly sweet, is most frequently ordered at Thai restaurants to please the children in the party (hence the name), but we have yet to serve it to an adult who didn't like it!

The hard-boiled eggs are a constant, but you can use other types of meat—beef or spareribs, for example.

5	cloves garlic	5
4	fresh coriander roots	4
1 tsp	ground black pepper	5 mL
4 cups	water	1 L
6	pieces of chicken (thigh, leg or breast) (approx 1 lb/500 g)	6
4 tbsp	fructose	60 mL
5 tbsp	fish sauce	75 mL
4 tbsp	dark soya sauce	60 mL
1 tsp	salt	5 mL
6	hard-boiled eggs	6
6	pieces deep-fried tofu (1 lb/500-gm tub before deep-frying)	6

In a mortar, pound garlic and coriander roots to a paste. Add ground pepper and pound or stir to mix.

In a heavy pot, combine garlic mixture, water and chicken pieces. Bring to the boil. Reduce heat a little and add fructose, fish sauce, soya sauce and salt.

Add hard-boiled eggs; boil gently 1 hour or until chicken is very tender and liquid is reduced by half. Add tofu. This dish can be prepared a day in advance and refrigerated. Reheat to serve. The eggs will turn very brown.

Serve with plain steamed rice. **Serves 6.**

TASTE
SWEET

NORTHERN-STYLE SPICY PORK DIP
Nam Prik Ong

Here's a great family-style dish. At dinner parties, it's as good an ice-breaker as fondue. Set out a plate of lightly steamed and raw vegetables and a bowl of sticky rice and invite your guests to eat with their fingers.

This is a good make-ahead or picnic dish. Serve warm or room temperature with crispy pork crackling and lightly steamed and/or raw vegetables such as eggplants, cabbage wedges, cucumber, coriander, fresh basil and carrots.

5	fresh coriander roots	5
4	cloves garlic	4
3	shallots	3
2 tbsp	light vegetable oil	30 mL
1 tbsp	Red Curry Paste (see page 104)	15 mL
10 oz	finely ground pork	300 g
1 cup	chopped tomatoes	250 mL
1 cup	water	250 mL
4 tbsp	fructose	60 mL
6 tbsp	fish sauce	90 mL
5 tbsp	tamarind puree	75 mL
2 tbsp	salt	30 mL

In a mortar, pound together coriander roots, garlic and shallots to a rough paste.

Heat oil in a wok; fry Red Curry Paste over medium heat 2 minutes. Add coriander root paste and stir-fry 2 minutes.

Add chicken and cook, stirring, until lightly browned and well mixed. Add tomatoes and water, bring to the boil. Reduce heat and boil gently 15 minutes.

Add fructose, fish sauce, tamarind puree and salt. Mix well and taste and adjust seasonings.

Simmer gently about 30 minutes more, or until the mixture has thickened considerably.

When the mixture has cooled completely, you can cover and store in the refrigerator for up to three days. Reheat before serving. **Serves 10 as an appetiser, 4 as a main dish.**

HEAVENLY BARBECUED CHICKEN
Gai Yang Sawaan

Here is a quick and easy barbecue dish that can be adapted to any meat (try it on venison or steak!). It's interesting to note that before 1507, when the first Portuguese traders introduced the North American chilli pepper plant to Thailand, the "hot" in Thai food came (as it does in this dish) exclusively from peppercorns. To tone down the "bite" of this dish, cut back on the peppercorns.

3 lb	whole chicken	1.5 kg
6	cloves garlic	6
2 tsp	salt	10 mL
2 tbsp	black peppercorns	30 mL
3	whole coriander plants, including roots	3
2 tbsp	lime juice	30 mL
6 tbsp	coconut cream	90 mL

Cut chicken into serving-size pieces.

Using a mortar and pestle, crush garlic with salt. Add peppercorns. Pound in the coriander plant and continue pounding until coarse. Add lime juice and coconut cream and blend to a thick paste.

Rub into chicken pieces, using a spoon or spatula as the peppercorns will cause skin to burn. Cover and let stand for at least 1 hour, or refrigerate overnight.

Broil or barbecue about 6 inches (15 cm) from heat, turning every 5 minutes, for about 25 minutes until skin is crisp and juices run clear when chicken is pierced. **Serves 5.**

TASTE
SLIGHTLY
SALTY

DRUNKARD'S STIR-FRY
Phad Kii Mau

The inflammatory nature of this dish is designed to get an alcohol-sodden system functioning again (if hung over). Served in the middle of an alcohol-heavy meal, it will, of course, speed the absorption of alcohol into the bloodstream.

Needless to say, your lips need never touch alcohol to enjoy this fiery dish—any chilli lover will be delighted with it!

8	finger-hot chillies	8
8	Thai bird chillies	8
3	cloves garlic	3
3	fresh coriander roots	3
2 tbsp	vegetable oil	30 mL
1-2 tbsp	Red Curry Paste (see page 104)	15-30 mL
7 oz	chicken, boned and cut into bite-sized pieces	200 g
7 oz	shrimp, peeled	200 g
1 tbsp	fish sauce	15 mL
1/2 tsp	fructose	2 mL
5	fresh Thai basil leaves	5

Garnish

> Green onions
> Chillies, sliced
> Sweet red pepper, sliced
> Coriander leaves

Bruise finger-hot chillies slightly, then slice lengthwise and set aside. Bruise or smash bird chillies, then pound to a paste in a mortar together with garlic and coriander roots.

Heat oil in a wok, add garlic mixture and stir-fry quickly about 1 minute, until it starts to give off its volatile oils—you'll start to cough! Add Red Curry Paste and stir-fry 2 minutes.

Add chicken, shrimp, finger chillies, fish sauce and fructose and stir-fry 3 minutes over high heat. Add basil leaves, stir-fry briefly just until leaves wilt. Remove to a serving plate. Garnish with green onions, chillies, sweet red pepper and fresh coriander leaves. Serve with lots of rice! **Serves 4.**

TASTE
HOT
HOT
HOT!

BASIL CHICKEN STIR-FRY
Gai Phad Baay Krapao

This classic and easy-to-make stir-fry depends on a supply of fresh Thai basil. European-style broad-leaved basil really doesn't make it in this dish. For this reason, I hesitate to include it in this cookbook, but when there is a ready supply of Thai basil, plan to cook this.

For a really interesting variation, substitute finely chopped fresh shrimp for chicken. This stir-fry will taste great whether you make it hot, mild or even without chillies.

1 lb	boneless chicken breasts	500 g
10	stalks fresh Thai basil	10
1	sweet red pepper	1
25	black peppercorns	25
3	garlic cloves	3
1	fresh coriander root	1
2 tbsp	light vegetable oil	30 mL
1 tbsp	fish sauce	15 mL
1 tbsp	fermented soya beans	15 mL
2 tsp	fructose	10 mL
1 tbsp	fresh chilli paste (or 4 finger-hot chillies, bruised then slivered for "hot" version if desired)	15 mL

Remove skin from chicken breasts and cut meat into julienne slivers.

Remove leaves from basil stalks, wash and set aside. Cut sweet red pepper in julienne slivers.

In a mortar, pound peppercorns, garlic and coriander root to a paste.

Heat oil in a wok or heavy-bottomed frying pan on high heat. Add peppercorn paste and stir-fry 1 minute. Add chicken and stir-fry until chicken turns white.

Add red pepper, fish sauce, fermented soya beans, fructose, and chilli paste, if desired; stir-fry 1 minute until bubbling. Stir in basil leaves and stir-fry 1 more minute or until leaves are wilted but still green.

Serve at once with steamed rice. **Serves 4.**

TASTE
SALTY
HOT
(IF DESIRED)

DEMON'S DARE
Nua Phad Prik

If you use shrimp, reduce cooking time by half.

We created this dish for those who wanted it hot, and have been surprised by how many take the dare—and even ask for it to be made extra hot!

In this quick and easy Thai mainstay, chilli peppers are not only the main spice but also one of the vegetables. Increase the number of chillies if you dare! To make the dish even hotter, increase the amount of crushed chillies as desired, and put them in the wok *first*. The longer they cook, the hotter they'll be.

This dish will serve four if served with other main dishes (a curry, a fish dish, noodles or a main course salad) or two if eaten by itself. Because it's so hot, it is a good idea to serve it with something mild. I would recommend stir-fried glass noodles with cabbage as a nice foil.

Have all ingredients ready as you'll be working very quickly. This dish will be ready to serve in 5 minutes.

2 tbsp	light vegetable oil	30 mL
2	cloves garlic, finely chopped	2
2	fresh coriander roots, crushed	2
2 tbsp	crushed red chillies, fresh or bottled	30 mL
14-16 oz	beef tenderloin, sliced (or large shrimp)	400-500 g
4 tbsp	water (or light broth)	60 mL
1 tbsp	fish sauce	15 mL
1 tsp	fructose (or other sweetener)	5 mL
1	small onion, sliced in thin wedges	1
4	fresh finger-hot chillies, sliced diagonally	4
12	fresh Thai basil leaves	12

Heat wok over high heat. Add oil and heat for a few seconds. Add garlic and stir briskly a few seconds. Add coriander root and chillies, and stir briefly. Add beef, stir-fry about 1 minute or until beef no longer looks raw. Add water, fish sauce and fructose, stir briefly, then bring liquid to a rapid boil.

Add onion and finger-hot chillies. Stir-fry until onions are slightly soft and clear. Add fresh basil leaves, stir to mix. Turn out on serving plate. **Serves 2-4.**

TASTE
HOT

NORTHERN-STYLE CHOPPED BEEF
Laab Issan

The true Northern Thai Laab calls for uncooked beef, a Thai Steak Tartare. Our version is cooked. Laab is traditionally served at room temperature.

Thais love to eat this dish fiery hot, with lots of raw or briefly steamed vegetables and sticky rice to cool the palate.

You can regulate the "heat" of this dish by using hotter or milder chillies as desired. If you want a mild dish, don't use fewer hot chillies—use milder ones. For a hotter dish use tiny Thai bird chillies and crush well before chopping.

1 lb	lean ground beef (or finely chopped round steak)	500 g
4 tbsp	roasted rice powder (see page 23)	60 mL
2 tsp	fresh chillies, finely chopped	10 mL
4 tbsp	fresh lime juice	60 mL
2 tbsp	fish sauce	30 mL
6-8	shallots, sliced	6-8
8	stalks fresh coriander, coarsely chopped	8
4	green onions, finely chopped	4
30	fresh mint leaves, coarsely chopped	30

Place ground beef in a strainer and cook, stirring, 2-3 minutes in rapidly boiling water or until no longer pink.

Drain and place in a mixing bowl. Mix in rice powder, chillies, lime juice, fish sauce, shallots, coriander, green onions and mint leaves. Adjust seasonings if necessary—dish should be hot, sour and salty.

Serve with raw vegetables and sticky rice. **Serves 4.**

TASTE
SOUR
SALTY
HOT

SIAMESE BEEF
Nua Yang

We served this tender, low-calorie beef dish as a lunch special for years. It was such a hit with the customers, we finally put it on the regular menu. It's a deceptively simple dish: the dipping sauce is what makes you sit up and take notice!

Steak

5	black peppercorns	5
2	cloves garlic	2
1	fresh coriander root	1
2 tsp	fish sauce	10 mL
1 tsp	light vegetable oil	5 mL
7-10 oz	lean beef steak	200-300 g
	Lettuce	

Sauce

2 tbsp	fish sauce	30 mL
2 tbsp	lime juice	30 mL
2 tsp	fructose (or other sweetener)	10 mL
1	clove garlic	1
2	shallots	2
1	hot chilli, or to taste	1
2	sprigs fresh coriander	2

Steak: In a mortar, pound peppercorns, garlic, coriander root, fish sauce and oil to a fine paste. Rub over the steak, cover and refrigerate 1 hour, or until ready to barbecue.

Sauce: Combine fish sauce, lime juice and fructose and stir well until fructose dissolves. Slice garlic and shallots very thinly and add to liquid. Chop chilli fine and add. Just before serving, chop coriander roughly and stir in.

Barbecue the marinated steak until done to your taste. Slice across the grain into fairly thin strips and arrange on a bed of lettuce. Garnish with raw or lightly steamed vegetables to taste and serve with the dipping sauce in a small bowl on the same dish. **Serves 1 or 2.**

TASTE

SWEET
SALTY
HOT
SOUR

BEEF STIR-FRIED WITH ROASTED CHILLI PASTE
Nua Phad Nam Prik Pau

This dish is so simple, yet so tasty, you'll want to try it with all manner of meats and serve it again and again.

You can really taste the tamarind in the thick sauce that clings so hotly to the meat.

1 lb	beef tenderloin	500 g
2 tbsp	vegetable oil	30 mL
2 tbsp	Roasted Chilli Paste (see page 114)	30 mL
1	medium cooking onion, slivered (optional)	1

Garnish

Fresh Thai basil leaves
Slivered red chillies

Slice beef tenderloin very thinly.

Heat oil in a wok over medium-high heat. Stir-fry beef until cooked, about 5 minutes. Add Roasted Chilli Paste and stir-fry over medium heat until beef is well coated.

Add slivered onion, if using, and stir-fry until onion is cooked but still crunchy.

Garnish with fresh basil leaves and red chillies and serve with plenty of steamed rice. **Serves 4 hot-food lovers.**

TASTE

HOT
SWEET
SOUR

*If you wish
the dish to be
VERY HOT,
add fresh chillies
with the beef.*

CHILLI BEEF
Nua Sub Phad Prik

Chilli Beef is so quick and easy to make, you'll want to serve it often. Variations can be made with any kind of meat or seafood.

When I make this for the children, I eliminate the chillies and basil leaves. I think they like it for its saltiness!

2-3 tbsp	vegetable oil	30-45 mL
3	cloves garlic, chopped	3
2	fresh coriander roots, pounded	2
1 lb	ground beef	500 g
1	medium onion, cut in wedges	1
8	fresh finger-hot chillies	8
2 tbsp	fish sauce	30 mL
15	fresh Thai basil leaves	15
1 tbsp	fructose	15 mL
2 tbsp	light soya sauce (optional)	30 mL

In a wok, heat 1 tbsp (15 mL) oil; stir-fry chopped garlic approximately 1 minute until golden. Add coriander roots and ground beef. Stir-fry for about 3 minutes.

Push ground beef up the side of the wok. Stir-fry the onion and chillies for 2 minutes, adding more oil if necessary.

Stir the ground beef back into the onion mixture. Add fish sauce, basil leaves, fructose, and soya sauce, if desired. Cook on high heat until a gravy forms and beef is no longer pink, 3-5 minutes.

Serve immediately with steamed rice. **Serves 4.**

T
A
S
T
E

HOT
SALTY

*PHOTO: Thai Rice Noodles [Phad Thai] (page 156)
shown with (clockwise from top left) rice vermicelli, bean thread noodles,
rice stick, rice vermicelli, dried wonton (egg) noodles, somen (wheat) noodles
and bean thread noodles in 50-gm bundles*

STIR-FRIED CURRIED PORK WITH GREEN BEANS
Muu Phad Prik Khing

There is a special "prik khing" curry paste for this, but you can use Red or Kua Curry Paste (see page 104 or 108).

This is a dish that is stunningly easy to prepare, and makes a big impact on your taste buds.

3 tbsp	vegetable oil	45 mL
2 tbsp	"prik khing" curry paste (can use Red or Kua)	30 mL
1/2 cup	water	125 mL
1 lb	pork tenderloin, thinly sliced	500 g
5	wild lime (makrood) leaves	5
14 oz	green beans, cut in 2-inch/5 cm lengths	400 g
1 tbsp	fructose	15 mL
3 tbsp	fish sauce	45 mL

Heat oil in wok; stir-fry curry paste about 10 minutes. Add water as curry paste dries. Add pork and lime leaves, stir-fry 5 minutes, until pork is no longer pink.

Add green beans and cook 5 minutes. Add fructose and fish sauce. Taste and adjust seasoning. Serve immediately. **Serves 4.**

PHOTO: Stir-fried Jade Greens (page 183)
shown with Thai fish sauce and fermented soya beans

If using dried lime leaves, add along with pork. If using fresh lime leaves, add with green beans.

T
A
S
T
E
SWEET
HOT

SIDE PORK WITH CRISPY CRACKLING
Khaep Muu

Make this to serve with Northern-style nam prik dips. If you want to enjoy this dish but haven't the time or inclination, a good substitute is chicken skin, deep-fried until light brown and crisp!

2 lb	fresh side pork from the belly, rind on	1 kg
1 tbsp	salt	15 mL
1 tbsp	peppercorns	15 mL
1	clove garlic, crushed	1
2	stalks fresh coriander, bruised	2
2 tbsp	vinegar	30 mL
1/2 cup	vegetable oil	125 mL

Put the pork rind, salt, peppercorns, garlic and coriander stalks into a medium pot of cold water. Bring to a boil. Simmer until the pork rind is tender. Remove the pork and trim the edges.

To make crackling, score the skin with a sharp knife along the length of the pork about 1 inch (2.5 cm) apart. Then score crosswise. Allow to cool.

Brush the skin with some vinegar and allow to dry. Repeat this a few times. Then bake pork in 325°F (180°C) oven about 40 minutes until skin is completely dry. Allow to cool on a rack several hours or overnight.

Cut the pork right through into strips. Heat the oil in a deep saucepan until just before the smoking point and deep-fry the pork strips until crisp and golden. Drain well on paper towel. Cut into tiny slices about the size of a fingernail. Serve with Northern-Style Spicy Pork Dip (see page 138), vegetables and sticky rice. Serves about 10.

TASTE
SALTY

GINGER PORK
Muu Phad Khing

This is a popular cold-weather dish. The ginger helps to heat the blood and aids and stimulates digestion.

The secret to this dish is to use the youngest, tenderest ginger you can find and cut it into fine matchstick shreds.

1 oz	cloud ear mushrooms	25 g
14 oz	pork loin	400 g
2 tbsp	vegetable oil	30 mL
2	cloves garlic, minced	2
2 oz	ginger, cut into fine matchstick shreds (about 4 in/10 cm)	50 g
1	cooking onion, cut in thin wedges	1
1 tsp	fermented soya beans	5 mL
1 tsp	fructose	5 mL
1 tbsp	oyster sauce	15 mL
1 tbsp	fish sauce	15 mL
3	green onions, cut diagonally in 2-inch/5 cm pieces	3
1	sweet red pepper, slivered	1

Soak cloud ear mushrooms 30 minutes in hot water. Drain and rinse well to remove all sand.

Cut pork into bite-sized chunks.

Heat oil in a wok over medium heat. Add garlic, stir briefly. Add pork, stir-fry until pork turns white, about 5 minutes.

Add ginger and onions and stir-fry 2-3 minutes. Add mushrooms, fermented soya beans, fructose, oyster sauce and fish sauce. Boil hard 3-5 minutes, until well blended and sauce is slightly reduced.

Add green onions and red pepper, stir-fry for 1 minute. Turn onto a platter and serve. **Serves 2-4.**

TASTE
SALTY

BANGKOK DUCK
Phet Phad Khing

Our local North American ducks taste just great when stir-fried in this Bangkok style.

This rich and very wonderful dish can be easy to make if you're willing to chop the duck up with the bones in. Even if you decide to take the high road and bone the duck completely, it's well worth the effort for this cold-weather dish.

1	young duck, about 3 lb/1.5 kg	1
7 oz	ginger root (about 14 in/35 cm)	200 g
5	green onions	5
1	onion	1
1	sweet red pepper	1
1	can (7 1/2 oz/213 mL) straw mushrooms	1
1	can (7 1/2 oz/213 mL) water chestnuts	1
2 tbsp	vegetable oil	30 mL
3	cloves garlic, minced	3
1 tbsp	oyster sauce	15 mL
1 tsp	fish sauce	5 mL
1 tbsp	fermented soya beans	15 mL
1 tsp	fructose	5 mL
5-6	celery leaves	5-6

Remove skin and fat from duck and discard. If desired, bone the duck as well, reserving bones to make soup. Cut the duck into bite-sized chunks with a meat cleaver.

Peel ginger root and cut into fine matchstick shreds. Cut green onions in 2 1/2-inch (7 cm) pieces, then lengthwise twice. Slice onion fairly thickly in wedges. Cut red pepper into julienne or triangles.

Drain straw mushrooms. Drain water chestnuts and cut each chestnut into 2 or 3 rounds.

Heat oil in a wok over high heat, add garlic and stir briefly. Add duck and stir-fry 3 minutes for small pieces, 6 minutes for large pieces. Add ginger and continue stir-frying another 3-6 minutes, until juice no longer runs pink when you prick the duck.

Add oyster sauce, fish sauce, fermented soya beans and fructose and continue cooking while you taste for seasoning, and adjust if necessary.

Add onion wedges, water chestnuts and straw mushrooms, and return to the boil. Add celery leaves, green onion and red pepper and cook 1 minute. **Serves 6**, when served with rice and other dishes.

TASTE
SALTY

CHAPTER 10
RICE AND NOODLES

Rice is the core of a Thai meal. It is important to choose a good rice and cook it perfectly. In Thailand, only white, polished rice is served. Every foreigner newly arrived in Thailand will ask about brown rice, for we have been taught to appreciate the importance of fibre and B vitamins. "Brown rice," the foreigner is told in no uncertain terms, "is for the army, the hilltribes—and the prisons."

Culinary snobbery aside, remember that the many vegetables in a Thai meal provide that all-important fibre, and the B vitamins will show up in the fish products—kapi, fish sauce, dried fish and dried shrimp.

The cooking of rice is such a personal thing that we don't agree among ourselves at Bangkok Garden how it should be cooked. I will give you three methods, and you can experiment to see which way you prefer.

Please bear in mind that all these measurements are relative, and may have to be varied depending on the age and variety of rice you are cooking. Allow between 1/2 and 1 cup (125-250 mL) uncooked rice per person.

See also Rice, pages 22-23.

Method 1: Steaming
This is the old-fashioned way and the one I prefer. It is also the method we use at Bangkok Garden, using a commercial steam convection oven instead of the multi-layered steamer (sung) I have at home.

Bring water to a rapid boil in the reservoir of the sung. Place rice to be cooked in the bowl you're planning to steam it in and wash 2 or 3 times under cold running water until the water runs relatively clear. Pour off most of the water, leaving enough on top to cover the rice. To determine if you have enough water, hold a finger straight down with the tip just touching the surface of the rice. The water should come just to the first knuckle.

Place the bowl in a sung layer (steamer), cover tightly and steam 20-30 minutes, until the rice has fluffed up and absorbed all of the water.

This method produces, for me, perfect rice every time, with each grain fluffy and separate.

Microwave Variation: Place bowl of rice and water in microwave. Cook on high 20-30 minutes. You may have to adjust cooking time according to wattage of microwave. I hate to admit it, but this produces rice just as fluffy as the other methods.

Method 2: Covered Saucepan

This method calls for water and rice in a ratio of slightly less than 2 measures water for each measure of rice (1 to 1 1/2 for newer crop rice). So for 8 people, use 4 cups (1 L) uncooked rice and 6-7 cups (1.5-1.75 L) water.

Wash rice first in cold water until water runs clear.

Combine rice and water in a saucepan and bring to a boil over high heat. Allow to boil rapidly, uncovered, about 10 minutes or until water just reaches the top of the rice. Cover tightly, reduce heat to low, cover and cook about 20 minutes or until all water is absorbed and each grain is fluffy.

Method 3: Electric Rice Cooker

Even the fussiest of Thai cooks will instantly praise the efficiency of an electric rice cooker. If you cook a lot of rice and you like a foolproof method of cooking, buy an electric rice cooker from an Oriental store—there are several good Japanese brands. You'll still have to wash the rice first, then measure rice and water into the cooker according to the manufacturer's specifications and—presto! Perfect rice every time!

STICKY RICE

First, make sure you have the right rice. Sticky rice is short-grained and very white and can be confused with Japanese rice. See Sticky Rice, page 23.

Soak sticky rice several hours or overnight in cold water. Rinse. Spread a clean cloth over the holes of a sung layer. Spread the washed rice evenly over the towel. Bring water to a rapid boil in the reservoir; cover tightly and steam 45 minutes, or until centre of rice grain is no longer hard. For proper cooking, the steam must flow over and around the grains. Some claim they have cooked sticky rice in a covered saucepan; I've tried this and all I get is a gluey mess.

Rice for Stir-Frying (Khaaw Phad):
Use cooked long-grain rice only. It should not be too soft or it will stick to the pan and burn. For best results, cook ahead of time and refrigerate, then fluff with a fork before stir-frying.

Sticky rice cannot be stir-fried.

NOODLES

It would be impossible to fairly represent the dozens of superb noodle dishes prepared by Thai street vendors and small market stalls. They have elevated noodle cookery to a high art. Perhaps it's for this reason that most Thais prefer to leave noodle cookery in the hands of the experts, and eat noodles mostly when away from the home. The following recipes make a wonderful addition to any Thai meal, and it's worth your while to learn to cook one or two of them.

See also Noodles, pages 19-21.

STEAMED CHICKEN RICE
Khaaw Mun Gai

Small food shops all over Thailand specialize in this easy lunch dish. The secret to its universal appeal seems to be the rich, satisfying flavour of rice steamed in a strong chicken broth. The side sauces add zest, and are optional, making this homey dish perfect for all ages, and even for invalids.

At home, we make a soup with the remaining broth by boiling onions, cauliflower chunks and whole black peppercorns about half an hour, until vegetables are tender.

1	whole chicken, 3-4 lb/1.5-2 kg	1
2	cooking onions, quartered	2
10-20	black peppercorns	10-20
1-2	stalks celery (optional)	1-2
16 cups	(approx) water	4 L
4 cups	uncooked rice	1 L
2	cloves garlic, bruised and finely chopped	2
1 tbsp	finely shredded ginger root	15 mL
3 tbsp	dark soya sauce (or bottled oyster sauce)	45 mL
1 tbsp	fermented soya beans	15 mL
Quarter	lemon (or lime)	Quarter
2 tbsp	fish sauce	30 mL
1	chilli pepper, finely chopped	1

Garnish

Sliced cucumber
Fresh coriander leaves
Green onions, chopped

Wash chicken well. Put in a pot with onions, peppercorns and celery, if desired. Cover with water, bring to boil, reduce heat and simmer until chicken is tender, at least 2 hours. Remove skin and bones; set aside chicken meat and keep warm. Strain the chicken broth and set aside.

Wash rice several times in running water. Drain, put in a bowl and cover with chicken broth, making sure you include as much of the fat as you can. (Use the same amount of chicken broth as you would water if you were making plain rice: hold your finger straight down with the tip just touching the surface of

TASTE

NEARLY
NEUTRAL

the rice and make sure the chicken broth comes just to the first knuckle.)

Steam in a rice steamer, 35-40 minutes, until rice fluffs up. The chicken fat will make the rice grains gleam.

Make a salty, gingery sauce by blending garlic, ginger, soya sauce, fermented soya beans and a squeeze of lemon or lime juice. Make a hot and salty sauce by blending fish sauce with chopped chilli and a squeeze of lemon or lime.

To serve, mound the rice on individual plates. Arrange chicken pieces on the rice and garnish generously with cucumber, coriander and green onions. Serve sauces on the side. **Serves 6.**

THAI RICE NOODLES
Phad Thai

There are as many versions of this dish as there are cooks! Bangkok Garden guests come long distances to eat Phad Thai for lunch. Phad Thai is starting to appear on the menus of restaurants of every price range and cuisine type.

If you're eager to add this rich tangy dish to your repertoire, be warned that it may take a bit of practise to get the knack of handling so many ingredients in a single pan.

Once you've mastered the art, you may want to personalize the dish, substituting chicken or bean curd, adjusting the chilli "bite," the sweetness or tartness of the noodles. Just remember there's one substitution that *can't* be made: the sour tamarind sauce that gives the dish its characteristic tang.

3.5 oz	dried rice noodles, medium-sized	100 g
4 tbsp	light vegetable oil	60 mL
2	cloves garlic, finely chopped	2
1 oz	raw shrimp, chopped	20 g
1 oz	ground pork	20 g
1 tsp	fructose (or other sweetener)	5 mL
2	eggs, beaten	2
2 tbsp	tamarind puree	30 mL
4 tbsp	fresh bean sprouts, roots removed	60 mL
1	stalk garlic chive, chopped	1
1 tbsp	chopped salted turnip	15 mL
1 tbsp	fish sauce	15 mL
1 tsp	soya sauce	5 mL
Pinch	pepper	Pinch

Garnish

2 tbsp	coarsely ground unroasted peanuts (see page 22)	30 mL
4 tbsp	fresh bean sprouts, roots removed	60 mL
4	slices cucumber	4
4-6	stalks garlic chives (or green onions)	4-6
2	wedges lemon (or lime)	2

To make this dish hot, add one or more teaspoons (5 mL) dried, powdered chillies after stir-frying bean sprouts.

T
A
S
T
E
SOUR
HOT
SALTY

Soak noodles in hot water until soft, about 2 minutes, then drain.

Heat wok until it smokes. Add oil, wait 1 minute, then fry the garlic briefly until golden. Add the shrimp, ground pork and fructose and stir-fry 1 minute, until pork turns brown. Pour in beaten eggs, cook until set slightly, then stir to scramble. Push this mixture up the sides of the wok.

Add the noodles and stir-fry for 2-3 minutes, until lightly browned. Push noodles up the sides of the wok. Add the tamarind puree and cook until it smokes, about 1 minute. Add bean sprouts, garlic chive and salted turnip and stir-fry until bean sprouts are slightly cooked, about 1 minute, adding fish sauce, soya sauce and pepper as you go. Stir noodles and egg-meat mixture down into tamarind mixture until well mixed.

Pile noodles on a serving dish and sprinkle with peanuts. Place piles of bean sprouts, cucumber slices, garlic chives and lemon wedges on the side of the plate. **Serves 1 as a main dish; 2 or more as a side dish.**

CRISPY NOODLES
Mee Grob

Finding the right noodles could well be the trickiest part of this dish. You need a thin rice noodle about the thickness of Italian angel hair pasta or bean thread noodles. These are sometimes called rice noodles, sometimes, unaccountably, rice stick. Make sure they are thin, and made of rice. At Bangkok Garden, we use a Thai brand called Erawan, in a clear cellophane package with green printing and a three-headed elephant logo.

You can also use bean thread noodles for this dish with very similar results. The bean thread noodles seem to absorb a little more oil than the rice noodles.

3 cups	vegetable oil for deep-frying (canola is best)	750 mL
5 oz	dried Thai rice vermicelli	150 g
2 oz	ground pork	50 g
2 oz	raw shrimp, peeled	50 g
1 tbsp	(approx) light vegetable oil	15 mL
2	cloves garlic, minced	2
1	shallot, finely chopped	1
1 tbsp	pickled garlic, finely chopped	15 mL
1	egg	1
3 tbsp	white vinegar	45 mL
3 tbsp	lime juice	45 mL
3 tbsp	tamarind puree	45 mL
4 tbsp	fish sauce	60 mL
4 tbsp	fructose	60 mL
2 tbsp	tomato ketchup	30 mL
3	green onions, cut in 1 1/4-inch/3 cm lengths	3
1/2 cup	bean sprouts, roots removed	125 mL
4 tbsp	fresh coriander leaves	60 mL
1 tbsp	finely shredded orange peel	15 mL

Garnish

6-12	whole cooked shrimp, tail on	6-12
1/2 cup	bean sprouts, roots removed	125 mL
6	stalks garlic chives	6
6-12	stalks fresh coriander	6-12
2	limes, cut in wedges	2

TASTE
SWEET
SOUR

Heat oil in a large wok on medium heat for about 10 minutes until oil swirls around in the pan and just begins to smoke.

Cut the noodles into manageable bunches with scissors. (Be prepared to work quickly and have a bowl ready to lift cooked noodles into.) Drop a generous handful of noodles into oil. They will hiss and puff up immediately. Turn them over at once, count to 10, then lift out into waiting bowl. Repeat until all noodles are fried. You'll have a large bowl of very crispy pale-gold noodles.

Chop ground pork with a sharp knife until it is very finely minced. Chop shrimp the same way.

In a wok, heat light vegetable oil, add fresh minced garlic, stir briefly, then add shallot and pickled garlic. Add pork and shrimp, stir well and cook 2 minutes over medium heat, until pork is browned. Beat egg with a little water. Add about one-third of the egg to the pork mixture, stirring vigorously.

Add vinegar, lime juice, tamarind puree, fish sauce, fructose and ketchup. Stir well and bring to the boil. Reduce heat slightly and simmer gently, stirring often, until sauce is thick and glossy and reduced by half, at least 10 minutes.

Meanwhile, in a separate pan, heat a little more oil and fry the remaining egg over high heat. Cool and cut the omelette into shreds.

To assemble, sliver green onions and combine with bean sprouts, coriander leaves, orange peel and shredded omelette. Sprinkle evenly over fried noodles in bowl.

To finish the dish, toss the noodle mixture lightly with the meat mixture. Use a spatula to avoid breaking up the noodles too much.

Mound onto a platter, garnish with cooked whole shrimp, bean sprouts, garlic chives, coriander stalks and lime wedges. Serves 1 as a main dish, 2 as a side dish.

BANGKOK NOODLES
Mee Gati

This noodle dish is rich and slightly sweet. Thais like to eat it with lots of chillies, garlic chives and crunchy raw veggies as a contrast.

You can vary the type of meat and fish used in the sauce according to your dietary requirements.

Sauce

1 1/2 cups	coconut cream	375 mL
1/2 cup	raw shrimp, peeled and chopped	125 mL
1/2 cup	ground pork	125 mL
1 tsp	chopped shallots	5 mL
1/4 tsp	chopped garlic	1 mL
1 tsp	fermented soya beans	5 mL
1 tsp	fish sauce	5 mL
1 tsp	fructose	5 mL
1 tsp	lime juice (or tamarind sauce or vinegar)	5 mL
1	unbeaten egg (optional)	1

Noodles

1 lb	Thai rice vermicelli	500 g
4 tbsp	vegetable oil	60 mL
Pinch	paprika (optional)	Pinch
6	plump red shallots, sliced into thin wedges	6
1 cup	bean sprouts, roots removed	250 mL
1 tbsp	fish sauce	15 mL
2 tsp	water	10 mL
1 tsp	chopped green onion tops	5 mL

Garnish

	Lettuce leaves or Chinese cabbage leaves	
	Fresh coriander leaves	
1	lemon (or lime), cut into wedges	1
	Fresh green (or red) chillies, to taste	
6	stalks garlic chives (or green onions), or to taste, left whole	6

TASTE

SWEET
SALTY

In saucepan, bring a few tablespoons of the coconut cream to a boil over medium heat. Add shrimp and pork; boil for a few minutes, stirring constantly. Reduce heat to simmer. Add the remaining coconut cream, shallots, garlic, fermented soya beans, fish sauce, fructose and lime juice. Simmer for about 10 minutes, stirring occasionally. Add the egg and stir until blended. Serve warm or at room temperature. This sauce can be prepared ahead and stored up to 3 days in the refrigerator.

Soak rice vermicelli in hot water about 5 minutes, until soft. Drain.

Heat the oil in a wok or frying pan over medium heat. Add the noodles. Stir and add paprika if desired to give them colour. Add shallots, bean sprouts, fish sauce, water and chopped green onions. Stir for a few minutes until everything is well blended.

Remove to a platter lined with lettuce leaves and pour the sauce over the noodles. Garnish with coriander leaves, lemon wedges, chillies and garlic chives. **Serves 2-4.**

ANYTIME NOODLES
Kwaytiaw Phad Laad-Naa

This dish is prepared in two parts, using the same wok. Have all ingredients ready before you start. The dish is cooked very quickly, you won't have time to look for anything or chop vegetables once you've started stir-frying.

We call this simple, everyday dish Anytime Noodles because it can be made in minutes, any time of the night or day, from ingredients you're sure to find in a Thai kitchen.

Traditionally, these noodles were made with beef (which sometimes had to be marinated in something because it was apt to be tough) but we make them with whatever protein appeals—chicken, egg, seafood or even pork loin.

The noodles can be made with or without gravy. Thais refer to this as "wet" or "dry" and usually add a scrambled egg to the dry version, regardless of the meat chosen.

You should find these wide, white noodles in any Chinese supermarket, and in some mainstream grocery stores.

For the "wet" version

2	chicken breasts	2
4 tbsp	light vegetable oil	60 mL
1 lb	fresh wide rice noodles	500 g
2 tbsp	dark soya sauce (or oyster sauce)	30 mL
2	small cloves garlic, bruised, then chopped	2
2-3 tbsp	fermented soya beans	30-45 mL
4	stalks Oriental mustard greens, cut diagonally in 2 1/2-inch/6 cm pieces	4
1 1/2 cups	chicken broth	375 mL
2 tbsp	oyster sauce	30 mL
4 tsp	fish sauce, or to taste	20 mL
4 tbsp	cornstarch	60 mL

Garnish

Grated carrot

Bone chicken breasts and make a light broth by boiling the bones and trimmings 30-45 minutes in 6 cups (1.5 L) of water. Cut meat into bite-sized pieces.

Heat the wok on high heat for 1-2 minutes. Add 2 tbsp (30 mL) oil, then add rice noodles, a handful at a time, stirring and tossing constantly. Sprinkle with dark soya sauce and stir-fry

TASTE

SALTY

until noodles are evenly coated. Remove to a warmed serving dish and arrange in an oval-shaped mound.

To the same wok, add remaining 2 tbsp (30 mL) oil and stir-fry garlic 30 seconds, until it begins to smoke and smell aromatic. Add chicken and stir-fry 3 minutes until no longer pink. Stir-frying constantly, add fermented soya beans, mustard greens, 3/4 cup (175 mL) of the chicken broth, oyster sauce and fish sauce. Cover and continue cooking 2 minutes at high heat, until greens are slightly cooked and bright green.

Add cornstarch dissolved in the remaining 3/4 cup (175 mL) broth. Continue cooking, stirring constantly, until gravy thickens.

Pour over noodles, garnish with a little grated carrot (for colour) and serve immediately. **Serves 2-4.**

For the "dry" version

Stir-fry noodles with soya sauce as for "wet" version. Remove. Add 2 or 3 eggs, to taste, to the wok and quickly stir-scramble; remove and set aside.

Add 2 tbsp (30 mL) oil to the wok and stir-fry chicken 2-3 minutes. Add greens, stir-fry briefly, then add 3/4 cup (175 mL) broth, oyster sauce and fish sauce. Continue stir-frying until some of the broth has evaporated and vegetables are cooked to desired crunchiness. Add cooked noodles and egg(s), stir briefly just until well mixed, and serve immediately.

This dish will not be completely dry—it just won't be accompanied by thick gravy. So don't feel you have to cook it until it's dried up.

Some Thais like to eat this with a little chilli vinegar on the side. (To make chilli vinegar, chop some fresh chillies and soak in white vinegar an hour.)

BANGKOK GARDEN'S NOODLE BAR: EGG NOODLES "DRY" WITH BBQ PORK
Bah Mee Haeng

In Thailand, dozens of delicious noodle dishes are prepared fresh and tailored to each customer's individual taste by street vendors from stationary or mobile carts. Street noodles are considered a hearty snack or light lunch, and are usually eaten between about 11 a.m. and dusk.

Thai street noodles are a legacy of the ethnic Chinese population who settled in Bangkok in the middle of the last century. In those days, noodle vendors loaded up a brass or wooden noodle stand with noodles, meats and condiments and a large soup kettle with a brazier below and carried these at either end of the flexible wooden pole through the streets, shouting out the menu. Customers would hail the vendor who would then set down his portable kitchen and whip up a dish of noodles finished to the customer's exact specifications.

In the last century, Chinese in Bangkok were subject to a nightly curfew and since all the original noodle vendors were Chinese, this dish was not available after dusk. To this day, street noodles are traditionally eaten during the day, to be replaced by the rice soups Khaaw Tom (see page 168) and Joke (see page 170) at night and in the early morning.

We have been serving Street Noodles in Bangkok Garden since the day the restaurant opened. They are enormously popular and, some say, addictive. They are not difficult to prepare at home, and are particularly good for busy families. You can prepare everything well ahead of time, then cook and finish everything in about 10 minutes. They're also great for big groups.

Fresh egg noodles are available in Oriental markets both fresh and vacuum packed. The ones we are talking about are thin (like angel hair pasta) and light brown, the colour of wonton wrappers. In fact, they may be called wonton noodles.

If you are not near a ready source of fresh Oriental noodles, you can use any type of thin, dried Oriental noodles, or fresh or dried Italian angel hair pasta. When using Italian pasta, be sure to cook it al dente.

The pork tenderloin is available in Chinese barbecue shops, where you can also purchase BBQ duck if you prefer. To make this pork at home, your Chinese supermarket will sell the powdered spices for marinating the meat. If none of these alternatives is available, substitute any type of meat, fowl or fish that appeals to you. Fish quenelles and shrimp quenelles (see page 120), whole or sliced, are good.

For pounded raw peanuts, buy fresh unroasted peanuts in their shells. Shell them, remove the papery skins and pound in a mortar until half of the peanuts are virtually powder while the other half are in chunks of varying sizes.

Salted turnip is available in vacuum packs in Oriental grocery stores. They are very salty and you may leave them out if you can't find them (or if you don't like the taste).

2 cups	fresh Oriental mustard green vegetable of your choice (about 8 stalks)	500 mL
2 cups	bean sprouts, roots removed	500 mL
2	green onions	2
7 oz	Chinese BBQ pork tenderloin	200 g
4 tsp	sliced salted turnip, or to taste	20 mL
8	stalks fresh coriander	8
4 tsp	fructose	20 mL
4 tbsp	pounded unroasted peanuts (see page 22)	60 mL
4 tbsp	Crispy Fried Garlic (see page 66)	60 mL
4 tbsp	fish sauce	60 mL
	Powdered hot chillies, to taste	
	Chilli vinegar (see page 47), to taste	
14-28 oz	fresh egg noodles	400-800 g

Soak Oriental green vegetable and bean sprouts in icy cold water to ensure maximum crispness.

Chop green onions. Slice pork tenderloin. Cut salted turnip into small dice or julienne. Pull leaves off coriander stalks; chop stalks into 2 1/2-inch (6 cm) lengths, then combine with leaves. Put onions, pork, turnip and coriander into separate bowls. Put fructose, peanuts, fried garlic, fish sauce, powdered hot chillies and chilli vinegar into individual bowls and set out on a tray or a counter ready to dress your noodles.

To Cook and Dress Noodles
Bring 8 cups (2 L) of water to boil in a large (at least 12 cup/3 L) pot. Bring 4 cups (1 L) of water to boil in another pot.

When water in smaller pot boils, drop in green vegetable and cook at a full rolling boil 3 minutes, until it turns bright

To make this into a noodle soup, pour 1 cup boiling chicken or pork stock over the noodles.

green but is still crunchy. Remove, drain, chop coarsely and set aside with other bowls of individual ingredients. Return water to boil.

Drop the noodles into the larger pot and cook in rapidly boiling water 3-4 minutes, or until noodles move easily but are still slightly al dente. (The water may foam up in the pot; to keep it from bubbling over, blow on the surface of the bubbles.) Remove from heat and drain.

While noodles are draining, drop bean sprouts into a smaller pot of boiling water and return to boil. Boil for 30 seconds until just blanched. Remove from heat and drain at once.

Divide the noodles among 4 large soup bowls or pasta plates. Add 1 tsp (5 mL) crispy fried garlic, 1 tbsp (15 mL) fish sauce, 1 tsp (5 mL) salted turnip, 1 tsp (5 mL) fructose, powdered hot chillies and chilli vinegar to taste. Using a fork and spoon, toss each serving until well mixed.

Arrange bean sprouts, green vegetables and pork tenderloin on top. Sprinkle with chopped green onions, fresh coriander stems and leaves and pounded peanuts. Serve immediately. Serves 4.

Noodle Condiments

At Bangkok Garden, "Noodle Bar" is a popular lunch. After building a bowl of "dry" or "soupy" noodles, we invite guests to adjust the seasonings themselves according to the five taste principle.

You may wish to do the same by setting out bowls of some or all of the following:

Chopped green onion
Chopped fresh coriander
Salted turnip, diced
Finely pounded peanuts (see page 22)
Chilli vinegar (see page 47)
Crispy Fried Garlic in Oil (see page 66)
Fish sauce
Powdered hot chillies
Fructose

Variations

Noodles

Sen Mee Lek: Thin rice noodles. If using fresh noodles, cook as for egg noodles. If using dried noodles, soak 10 minutes in hot water, then boil until al dente.

Sen Yai: These are the broad white rice noodles sold fresh in virtually any Chinese supermarket. They just need to be poached briefly in rapidly boiling water until they are slightly translucent. Slightly narrower rice noodles are available dried just about everywhere. Again, soak about 10 minutes in hot water before boiling.

Woon sen: These thin bean flour noodles are not as commonly served in this Noodle Bar style, but by all means consider doing so if you have guests who need to reduce the amount of carbohydrates they eat. Soak bean thread noodles 5-10 minutes in warm water, then cook in rapidly boiling water until tender and completely transparent, about 5 minutes.

Meat
Many meats, barbecued or plain, go well with Noodle Bar. Try:
    Chinese BBQ duck
    Steamed or boiled chicken
    Plain pork tenderloin, baked or steamed

    OR

    Tofu, plain or deep-fried
    Small fish, crisply deep-fried
    Fish or shrimp quenelles (see page 120)

"MIDNIGHT SOUP"
Khaaw Tom

*If you have
no cooked
chicken meat,
boil a chicken
breast along
with the rice,
then remove,
bone, shred and
return to pot.*

On my first long-distance bus trip in Thailand I was astonished when, at precisely midnight, the bus pulled up under a huge tamarind tree in the middle of nowhere. We were all shepherded off the bus and invited to sit at wooden picnic tables, where we were served bowls of hot rice soup, laced with garlic, fresh herbs and bits of chicken. I was soon to discover that this is a universal midnight snack all over Thailand. The seasonings remain the same, but the meats and vegetables change according to the region. I will never forget the bowl of Khaaw Tom I ate in a fishing village on the Thai isthmus on the way to the south: brimful of miniature sea creatures—shrimp, squid, fish—none more than half the size of my thumb!

We don't serve Midnight Soup any more at Bangkok Garden because it really is a snack—too hearty to serve with a meal but not hearty enough to be a meal in itself. At home, this makes a particularly good meal for an invalid, or for fussy children who want to control everything that goes into their mouths.

And if you have all the ingredients on hand, it's about the quickest and simplest Thai dish to prepare.

Offer Thai condiments such as crushed peanuts, powdered dried chillies, fructose, fish sauce, chilli vinegar and so on for your guests to adjust the seasonings according to their preferences.

1/2 cup	uncooked rice	125 mL
8 cups	light soup stock (or water or 8 cups/2 L water and 2 bouillon cubes)	2 L
7 oz	cooked chicken breast	200 g
2	green onions	2
8	stalks fresh coriander	8
4 tbsp	Crispy Fried Garlic in Oil (see page 66)	60 mL
4 tbsp	fish sauce	60 mL
	Chilli vinegar (see page 47), to taste	

Rinse rice once. Combine rice and stock in a heavy saucepan, bring to the boil and boil hard 20-30 minutes, stirring constantly for first 5 minutes, then occasionally to prevent sticking. Soup is ready when rice is soft but still in individual grains, and broth is slightly cloudy.

TASTE

DRESS IT
AS YOU
LIKE IT!

Shred chicken meat and add to stock. Chop green onions fine. Remove leaves from coriander, chop stalks, combine and set aside.

Divide soup into 4 large bowls. Add 1 tbsp (15 mL) crispy fried garlic, 1 tbsp (15 mL) fish sauce and chilli vinegar if desired to each bowl. Stir well. Sprinkle with green onions and fresh coriander and serve immediately. **Serves 4.**

Variations: Add any meat, fish or seafood to this soup, as you desire. For a heartier snack, increase the amount of protein to 3.5 oz/100 g per person. Try shrimps, scallops, fish or shrimp quenelles (see page 120), spareribs, duck, leftover turkey, shreds of omelette or bean curd.

Although the Thais don't do this, you might consider serving Midnight Soup with Sweet and Salty Air-Dried Beef (see page 54) and/or a "yum" salad (Chapter 6).

Variation: Blanched Pork Liver for Midnight Soup:
Pork Liver will add "bitter" taste. Thais like to eat this soup with pork liver. It is important not to overcook the liver, or it will be tough. On the other hand, you can't just drop pieces of raw liver into the boiling soup as the liver will "run" and discolour the broth.

To seal the liver, bring 2-3 cups (500-750 mL) of water to a rapid boil and add 4 oz (120 g) thinly sliced liver. Remove from heat at once. Stir liver pieces in the water until they turn light— about 1 1/2 minutes. Drain and set aside until ready to serve the soup. Add back into the soup at the last minute and serve immediately.

Time-saver variation:

1 1/2 cups	leftover cooked rice	375 mL
7 oz	cooked meat (or fish), shredded	200 g
4 tbsp	chopped fresh coriander	60 mL
4 tbsp	fish sauce	60 mL
4 tbsp	Crispy Fried Garlic in Oil (see page 66)	60 mL
4 tsp	chopped green onion	20 mL
	Chilli vinegar (see page 47), to taste	
6 cups	water (or light soup stock)	1.5 L

Divide the rice into 4 large bowls. Evenly divide meat, coriander, fish sauce, crispy fried garlic, green onion and chilli vinegar among bowls.

Bring water or soup stock to a rolling boil. Pour 1 1/2 cups (375 mL) over rice mixture in each bowl, stir to mix and serve immediately. **Serves 4.**

BREAKFAST RICE SOUP
Joke

This thick, comforting soup is made all over the Orient from Bombay to Seoul, and is the only real breakfast dish in Thai cuisine.

Thais will generally eat anything for breakfast, from sweet pastries and steamed or fried doughnuts to curries, either left over or purchased fresh from the market or from the local street vendor.

Omelettes are just as likely to find their way to the dinner table as to the breakfast table, but one item that is served exclusively in the mornings is Joke. Thick, rich and hearty, it is intended to be served very mildly spiced and dressed by the individual diner. It takes 45 minutes or more to make this soup, and you must start with uncooked rice.

Most people like to break a raw egg into the soup, allow it to coddle for a minute, then stir it into the soup. Personally, I prefer tiny meatballs made of chicken flavoured with garlic, coriander root and pepper.

This is a wonderful tonic for the ill or the convalescent.

| 1 cup | uncooked rice | 250 mL |
| 18 cups | water (or light stock) | 4.5 L |

Rinse rice once, then bring to the boil with 10 cups (2.5 L) of the water in a large saucepan. Boil hard 15 minutes, stirring constantly for the first 5 minutes, then occasionally to prevent sticking. Reduce heat until the soup is simmering and cook 30 minutes, stirring occasionally, until rice breaks down and soup becomes thick and white. Add more water as soup becomes thick. The amount of water you add depends on a number of factors, including how old the rice is and how thick you like your soup. I prefer a thick porridge.

Meanwhile, prepare condiments:
  Chopped green onions
  Chopped fresh coriander
  Chilli vinegar (see page 47)
  Fish sauce
  Diced salted turnip
  Pounded unroasted peanuts (see page 22)
  Powdered hot chillies
  Tiny deep-fried crispy fish
  Tiny deep-fried dried shrimp
  Crispy Fried Garlic in Oil (see page 66)
  Crispy fried shallots

TASTE

DRESS IT
AS YOU
LIKE IT!

Select and prepare a protein component. Some suggestions:
> Shreds of cooked meat
> Chunks of canned tuna
> Tiny meatballs
> Fish or shrimp quenelles (see page 120)
> Raw egg
> Hard-boiled egg or salted egg, quartered
> Steamed firm-fleshed fish
> Bean curd

Arrange protein component on a platter, and condiments on a tray. Serve bowls of plain rice soup and invite diners to flavour according to their own taste. **Serves 4.**

Chef Lek's no-fail shortcuts:
Put 2 cups (500 mL) cooked rice in a blender. Add 2 cups (500 mL) water and blend about 2 minutes. Return to the pot, add 2-4 cups (500 mL-1 L) water or light soup stock and boil gently, stirring occasionally to prevent sticking, about 15 minutes or until desired "porridge" consistency is reached.

If you don't have cooked rice: wash 1 cup (250 mL) rice and boil hard in 3 cups (750 mL) water for 15 minutes. Put in blender, blend 2 minutes. Return to pot, add 3 cups (750 mL) or more water and continue cooking and adding water or stock until desired "porridge" consistency is reached. This should take approximately 15 more minutes. **Serves 4.**

CHICKEN AND SHRIMP FRIED RICE
Khaaw Phad Gai Leh Kung

This is a hefty portion intended for up to four people. Using the method described below, you can create your own personal fried rice with fresh and leftover ingredients from your fridge.

1 lb	raw shrimp	450 g
3/4 lb	whole boneless chicken breasts, skinned	350 g
3	cloves garlic	3
2	medium cooking onions	2
1 cup	mixed vegetables (snowpeas, broccoli, cauliflower, corn, carrots, squash, shredded cabbage)	250 mL
Half	sweet red pepper	Half
Half	sweet green pepper	Half
6	green onions	6
2-3 tbsp	light vegetable oil	30-45 mL
2	eggs	2
4 cups	cooked white rice (cold)	1 L
5 tbsp	fish sauce, or to taste	75 mL
1-2 tsp	fructose, to taste	5-10 mL

Garnish

Tomato wedges
Cucumber slices
Fresh coriander sprigs
Carrot rounds
Lemon or lime wedges

Wash shrimp. Remove shells, leaving tails on. Cut chicken into bite-sized chunks. Smash garlic with the flat blade of a knife, then chop finely. Cut cooking onions into quarters, then cut quarters into thinner wedges.

Blanch mixed vegetables briefly in rapidly boiling water. Drain. Cut red and green peppers in lengths. Cut green onions in half crosswise. Set aside white halves for garnish; slice green tops diagonally in 2-inch (5 cm) lengths.

Heat 1 tbsp (15 mL) oil in a large wok over medium heat. Beat eggs well, pour into wok, allow to set 1 minute, then scramble. Remove from wok and set aside.

TASTE

SWEET
SALTY

In same wok, add 1 tbsp (15 mL) oil and chicken pieces. Stir-fry 3 minutes or until chicken is uniformly white. Add shrimp and garlic and stir-fry 2 or 3 minutes until shrimp curl and turn pink.

Add rice, cooking onions and mixed vegetables; stir-fry 3 minutes. You may wish to add a little more oil at this point.

Add red and green peppers and green onion tops; stir-fry 1-2 minutes, until green onions wilt but are still bright green.

Turn heat off and stir in scrambled egg, fish sauce and fructose. Taste and adjust seasoning.

Turn out onto a platter or 4 individual plates. Garnish with tomato, cucumber, coriander sprigs, carrots and lemon or lime wedges. Serve with chilli vinegar (see page 47) or chillies in fish sauce on the side. **Serves 4.**

EGG AND CRABMEAT FRIED RICE
Khaaw Phad Puu

Fried rice is a universal favourite for Thais of all ages—as a meal or a snack, any time of the night or day.

This is a perfect dish for leftover rice, as it must be cooked and cold for best results.

9 oz	crabmeat	260 g
3	cloves garlic	3
2	medium cooking onions	2
1	sweet red pepper	1
5	green onions	5
2	eggs	2
2 tbsp	light vegetable oil	30 mL
4 cups	cooked white rice (cold)	1 L
5 tbsp	fish sauce	75 mL
1-2 tsp	fructose	5-10 mL

Garnish

Lemon or lime wedges
Cucumber slices
Carrot, cut in rounds
Fresh coriander sprigs

Shred crabmeat. Crush garlic with the flat blade of a knife, then chop fine. Cut cooking onions in quarters, then slice the quarters into thin wedges. Cut red pepper into 2 1/2-3 inch (6-8 cm) lengths. Cut green onions in half crosswise. Reserve the white halves for garnish; chop the green halves diagonally in 2-inch (5 cm) lengths.

Heat a large wok over medium heat. Beat eggs well. Pour 1 tbsp (15 mL) oil into wok, pour in egg, allow to cook without stirring 1 minute, then scramble. Remove from wok and set aside.

In the same wok, add 1 tbsp (15 mL) oil and crabmeat and stir 1 minute. Add garlic and stir-fry 3 minutes or until crab is cooked. Add cooking onions and rice, stir-fry over medium-high heat until well mixed. Some people like to add a little more oil at this point. Add red pepper and green onions and stir about 2 minutes, until onions are wilted but still bright green.

Add cooked eggs, fish sauce and fructose and stir to mix. Taste and adjust seasoning. Put on 4 individual plates or mound on a platter.

TASTE
SWEET
SALTY

Garnish with reserved green onion, lemon wedges, cucumber slices, carrot rounds and sprigs of fresh coriander.

Serve Chilli Vinegar (see page 47) or chopped chillies in fish sauce on the side for those who like it hot. **Serves 2-4.**

STIR-FRIED GLASS NOODLES
Phad Woon Sen

Glass noodles—woon sen—are known as the "diabetic's noodles" because they are made from high-protein, low-carbohydrate mung bean flour and do not elevate the blood sugar rapidly during digestion.

This dish has become a staple in my home as it can be quickly prepared with whatever ingredients we have at hand: chicken, meat, shellfish or perhaps an egg and some green vegetable.

You'll be surprised at how well this dish serves to round out a Thai meal. I often include it when I'm serving a very hot dish as its soothing blandness is an excellent coolant.

1/2 lb	bean thread noodles (5 bundles)	250 g
3 tbsp	vegetable oil	45 mL
1/4 lb	pork tenderloin, cut in 1/2-inch/1 cm pieces (or minced)	125 g
1	clove garlic, minced	1
3	eggs, lightly beaten	3
2	green onions, cut into 1-inch/2.5 cm pieces	2
2 tsp	soya sauce	10 mL
2 tbsp	fish sauce	30 mL

Garnish
1 tbsp	fresh coriander leaves	15 mL
1 tsp	ground black pepper	5 mL

Soak bean thread noodles in hot water for 5 minutes, then drain well. They will be very soft and slippery.

Heat oil in a wok and fry pork over medium-high heat until light brown. Add the garlic and stir-fry for 30 seconds. Add beaten eggs, let them set slightly, then cook, stirring, until set. Add bean thread noodles, green onions, soya sauce, fish sauce, and stir-fry 2-3 minutes. Garnish with fresh coriander leaves and ground pepper. **Serves 4.**

TASTE
SALTY

BAKED PINEAPPLE RICE
Khaaw Op Sapparot

I'm not sure why this popular dish is called "baked" as it's usually served piping hot direct from the wok! You need to bake the
finished product only if you want to make the dish ahead.

The half pineapple presentation makes a pretty addition
to your dinner table. Children also love this dish; for them,
leave out the chilli and substitute fresh shrimp for dried.

1	whole pineapple	1
2 tbsp	dried shrimp	30 mL
1	clove garlic	1
1	shallot	1
1	fresh chilli	1
2	stalks fresh coriander	2
2 oz	ham	50 g
2 tbsp	vegetable oil	30 mL
3 cups	cooked rice	750 mL
2 tsp	fish sauce	10 mL
1 tbsp	Maggi™ sauce (or light soya sauce)	15 mL
Pinch	pepper	Pinch

Garnish

10	stalks fresh coriander, leaves only	10
10	slices of cucumber	10

Cut pineapple in half lengthwise through the crown. Do not
remove leaves. Hollow out, remove core, slice half the flesh for
garnish, chop remaining flesh and set aside in a bowl (scrape
the juice into the bowl too). Add dried shrimp.

Bruise garlic, then chop. Chop shallot, chilli and coriander;
shred ham. Heat a wok, add oil and briefly stir-fry garlic, shallot and chilli. Add rice and stir-fry 2 minutes at high heat. Add
fish sauce, Maggi™ sauce and pepper, stir-fry 1 minute longer.

Remove from heat, add pineapple mixture, coriander and
ham, mix well and pile into pineapple halves. (If you're planning to serve this directly without baking, continue to stir-fry 2
minutes, until pineapple is warmed through.)

Bake in 375°F (190°C) oven 15 minutes. Serve garnished
with coriander leaves, cucumber and pineapple slices.
Serves 2-4.

T
A
S
T
E

SWEET
SOUR
SALTY

CHAPTER 11
VEGETABLES

* * * * * * * * *

Many people think that because Thailand is such a devoutly Buddhist country, the food should be largely vegetarian. While vegetables are more important than meat in the Thai diet, soups, stir-fries, curries and noodle dishes will probably all contain *some* meat—even though the vegetables form the bulk of the dish.

And what magnificent vegetables they are, in a riotous variety of exotic, tasty plants unheard of in the West. Many have no English names: satoh beans and pods, kathin leaves, cha-om, rakam. There's pak bung, a tasty water spinach, and fresh banana flowers, which make a magnificent curry. There are fresh bamboo shoots, picked daily during the rainy season when they sprout vigorously like asparagus. A number of mustard greens or mustard cabbages, members of the brassica family, appearing daily in the markets, are mainstay stir-fried vegetables. Melons, marrows, cucumbers and pumpkins are favourite curry vegetables. Green mangoes, papayas and guavas can be prepared and served as either fruits or vegetables.

At first glance, it would seem that it is impossible to reproduce Thai food so far away from a source of tropical vegetables. But don't despair. Although we will never be able to reproduce the entire range of Thai cuisine spice for spice and leaf for leaf when we live two climatic zones and half a world away, there are many dishes that can be made with vegetables common to numerous climates round the world.

Certain Thai favourites such as bamboo shoots, water chestnuts, baby corn and straw mushrooms can be canned successfully and are available any time on your grocer's shelf. Tomatoes, eggplant, cucumbers, fresh mung bean sprouts, snow peas, long beans, snap beans, shallots, peppers sweet and hot, leaf lettuce and white radish are all popular Thai vegetables that can be found fresh in any market. Marrows such as summer squash and zucchini can substitute for Thai marrows, and butternut and acorn squash are similar to the firm-fleshed Thai pumpkin.

Broccoli, always a popular vegetable, though hard to grow in Thailand, is ideal for stir-frying; the art is in the proper cutting of it. Temperate-climate vegetables such as cauliflower, carrots and potatoes are also favoured in Thailand whenever available.

In short, though you may not be able to prepare *every* Thai vegetable dish in your North American kitchen, you can certainly make a wide range of authentic Thai vegetable dishes using vegetables you don't have to go farther than your supermarket to purchase.

I should also point out that most dishes in this book can be made vegetarian simply by eliminating the meat if a small amount is called for, or substituting vegetables for the meat—for example, in curries.

The classic Thai stir-fried vegetable dish is simple: ingredients perfectly cut and stir-fried in light vegetable oil over intense heat with garlic, fish sauce, a little pepper. Coriander root, a spoonful of fermented soya beans, shrimp paste or kapi, a dash of sugar if the vegetable is bitter are familiar optional additions to stir-fried vegetables.

The real art of Thai vegetable cookery is in the careful cutting of the vegetables. To cook properly, they should be of uniform size. If several vegetables are used, choose ones that either contrast with or complement each other in colour, flavour or texture and cut them in complementary or contrasting sizes and shapes.

Use a very sharp knife to prepare your vegetables; the smooth feel of a well-cut vegetable on the tongue is an important part of the experience of the dish. Vegetables that vary in texture make good stir-fry partners: contrast the crisp crunch of a tender snow pea with the softness of a vegetable marrow or a mushroom. You may not think of carrots as being very Thai, but do think of a few slivers or rounds of carrot to add colour to a vegetable dish.

Your vegetable dishes should follow the seasons, making use of what's freshest at your local market. In particular, don't miss the asparagus season! It makes the most wonderful stir-fried dish.

Choose vegetables that are firm and healthy. If you see one of the Oriental mustard greens or cabbages looking a little wilted, it's okay to buy it as long as the edges of the leaves are not dried out. Soak the leaves for a few hours in cold water. Most brassicas usually revive completely with this treatment: even the flowers will perk right up.

Because vegetables appear so extensively in all Thai dishes, Thais do not tend to concentrate their efforts on creating dishes centring specifically around vegetables. But when they do, the results are spectacular, as in Stuffed Tomatoes or Deep-fried Stuffed Eggplant, both of which have played to rave reviews at various Bangkok Garden festivals.

The simplest way of preparing vegetables for a Thai meal is to steam them lightly and serve with a fiery nam prik, or dipping sauce. Making a fine nam prik is one of the highest of Thai culinary arts, and if a cook is skilled in nam prik preparation, he or she is highly regarded. I've chosen just two from the many dozens of traditional nam prik for you to try. Serve them with steamed and raw vegetables, and sticky rice if you like.

The variety of stir-fried dishes it's possible to prepare should be limited only by your supplies and your imagination.

I hope these few recipes will inspire you to cook *all* your vegetables the Thai way. It's healthier, faster, more attractive—and best of all, tastier than any other method of vegetable preparation I've ever encountered.

STIR-FRIED BAMBOO SHOOTS
Phad Noh Maay

Although they are available the year round, bamboo shoots are traditionally associated with the rainy season when they shoot upward with such fury that they must be harvested early in the morning while they are still tender. It's easy to miss the right moment to harvest bamboo shoots: fuelled by damp heat and rains they can shoot up 10 inches (25 cm) in a single day.

Bamboo shoots are harvested by cutting them at the base with a sharp knife, the same as asparagus. There are two stages that yield a delectable vegetable. The first is when the shoots are small spears resembling pale asparagus. In the second stage, only hours later, the shoots are better developed, triangular in shape and slightly fibrous. As soon as they are harvested, they are immersed in a light salt brine, which preserves them and softens any tough fibrous parts.

You should boil bamboo shoots 10 minutes to draw out excess brine, then discard the boiling water.

Asparagus so resembles bamboo shoot in its growing habit that the Thai word for asparagus translates as "foreign bamboo shoot." In asparagus season, I like to mix the two together in a bilingual culinary pun.

I like bamboo shoots for their tender smooth feel on the tongue and their ability to stand up to the high heats required for stir-frying or currying.

If you like your food hot, you'll be glad to know that bamboo shoots intensify the "hot" of chillies when the two are combined in a dish. Try a hot Red Curry of Chicken (see page 106) with bamboo shoots and you'll see what I mean.

Bamboo shoots are sold canned in light brine. The label will tell you whether they are the spear-shaped first shoots or the slightly older, triangular shoots. This recipe calls for the tender young shoots cut into strips; another favourite method is to cut the older shoots into triangles, following the shape of the vegetable. It produces a very different result.

Use any kind of contrasting vegetable with bamboo shoots; a nice combination we often serve at Bangkok Garden is bamboo shoot triangles with carrot rounds and snow peas.

TASTE
SALTY
SWEET

1	can (14 oz/398 mL) spear-shaped bamboo shoots	1
1	sweet red pepper	1
4	green onions	4
2	cloves garlic	2
2	fresh coriander roots	2
3 tbsp	vegetable oil	45 mL
2 tbsp	fish sauce	30 mL
	Pepper, to taste	
1 tsp	fructose	5 mL
	Fresh coriander leaves, for garnish	

Drain brine from bamboo shoots, and slice lengthwise in strips. Boil bamboo shoots in water for 10 minutes. Drain. Cut red pepper and green onions into strips similar to bamboo shoots. Smash garlic with the flat blade of a knife and pound together with coriander roots.

Heat oil in a wok over high heat until oil begins to smoke; quickly stir-fry the garlic-coriander paste. Add green onions, stir-fry briefly, then add red peppers and toss a few times.

Add bamboo shoots, fish sauce, pepper and fructose, stir-fry until well mixed, cover and cook 1 minute. Taste and adjust the seasonings. Add a splash of water if needed.

Garnish with fresh coriander leaves and serve immediately. Serves 4.

Use firm-fleshed green vegetables in season for this typical Thai dish: broccoli, any of the Oriental mustard greens, Swiss chard, asparagus or green beans.

Some cooks like to add a tablespoon (15 mL) of fermented soya beans to a stir-fried vegetable along with the fish sauce. This increases the saltiness and adds a certain body to the dish.

T
A
S
T
E
SALTY

STIR-FRIED GREEN VEGETABLES WITH SHRIMP
Pak Phad Namaan Hoy

This is our basic recipe for stir-fried vegetables. The oyster sauce is optional and in fact we don't use it at Bangkok Garden. Have all ingredients lined up and ready to go, as this dish will taste best if you work quickly.

5	cloves garlic	5
3 cups	green vegetables, cut on the diagonal into 1-inch/2.5 cm lengths	750 mL
3 tbsp	vegetable oil	45 mL
1 tbsp	fish sauce	15 mL
1 tbsp	oyster sauce (optional)	15 mL
12	small raw shrimp, tail on	12

Bruise garlic well by smashing with the flat blade of a knife before finely chopping. Soak vegetables in ice water for 15 minutes to ensure they are really crisp.

Heat the wok over high heat until it just starts to smoke. Add oil, and stir-fry garlic briefly just until it changes colour.

Drain ice water from vegetables but do not shake. Add to wok and stir-fry over high heat for 3 minutes. Add fish sauce and a little water or broth if necessary. Cover and simmer for 3 minutes. Add oyster sauce, if using, and shrimp, and stir-fry until shrimp are just pink. Serve immediately. **Serves 4.**

STIR-FRIED JADE (MUSTARD) GREENS
Phad Khaa-Naa

Oriental mustard greens make a wonderful stir-fry and you're sure to find at least one variety in a store near you.

To achieve the desired results, remember to keep the heat high throughout the very short cooking process.

1 lb	Oriental mustard greens	500 g
	(about 4 cups/1 L chopped)	
2 tbsp	light vegetable oil	30 mL
2	cloves garlic	2
1 tbsp	fish sauce	15 mL
	Water, as needed	
1 tbsp	fermented soya beans (optional)	15 mL
	Pepper, to taste	

Using a sharp knife, trim the mustard greens and chop coarsely, cutting the crispy stems in lengths along the diagonal. Place in a bowl of cold water until ready to stir-fry. Just before cooking, drain mustard greens in colander but do not shake.

Heat wok or heavy-bottomed frying pan on high heat for 30 seconds. Add oil and heat 30 seconds.

Smash garlic with the flat blade of a knife and add to the oil. Stir a moment, then add mustard greens, thick stems first, leaves last, and stir-fry until wilted. The water clinging to the greens should boil immediately, causing steam to billow up from the wok. In Oriental cookery, this is known as "first steam."

Add fish sauce. Add water only if necessary (if none remains from the "first steam") and cover immediately to trap the steam and bathe the greens briefly (about 2 minutes) in a moist heat.

Stir-fry at high heat as you add soya beans, if using, until blended. If all liquid is gone, add another splash of water. Remove from heat, season with pepper and serve immediately. Serves 4.

Most Thai cooks would be unable to resist adding a handful of shrimp or some chicken or beef. If you wish to follow suit, add meat right after the garlic and push it up the sides of the pan to make room for the greens. You may need an extra tablespoon/15 mL of oil as well.

The vegetable referred to in this recipe has a green stem about the thickness of a finger, long oval dark green leaves and (sometimes) yellow flowers. Other Oriental greens of the brassica (mustard and cabbage) family can be substituted.

TASTE
SALTY

DEEP-FRIED STUFFED EGGPLANT
Makua Yatsai

Because of its meat content, this could just as easily be a main course dish.

At Bangkok Garden, it appears on festival menus as an appetiser.

1	strip bacon	1
10 oz	ground pork	300 g
3.5 oz	raw shrimp, peeled, deveined and finely chopped	100 g
1	egg yolk	1
2 tsp	soya sauce	10 mL
1/2 tsp	ground white pepper	2 mL
1	medium carrot, grated	1
1	medium onion, finely chopped	1
1 tsp	salt	5 mL
4	long, thin eggplants	4
1-2 cups	vegetable oil for deep-frying	250-500 mL
	Lettuce leaves	

Batter		
4-6	egg yolks	4-6
1/2 tsp	white pepper	2 mL
1 tsp	salt	5 mL
	Cornstarch	

Chop the bacon strip very fine. Combine bacon, pork, shrimp, egg yolk, soya sauce, white pepper, carrot, onion and salt in a bowl and stir until thoroughly mixed.

Wash eggplants and make a cut in the centre. Hollow out a depression big enough to hold one quarter of the meat mixture. Push meat mixture into the hollowed-out eggplants.

Batter: Measure egg yolks before pouring into a deep, wide bowl; beat about 1 minute. Add pepper, salt and an amount of cornstarch equal to the eggs. Stir vigorously until ingredients are well combined.

In a wok, heat oil over medium heat. Coat stuffed eggplant thoroughly with batter, put immediately into hot oil, stuffing

While deep-frying, keep eggplants stuffing side up and handle gently. The batter helps to hold the stuffing onto the egg-plant halves, and with care-ful handling it all stays together.

If only the large purple oval-shaped eggplants are available, cut one in half lengthwise, hollow out depressions and fill each with half the meat mixture.

TASTE
SALTY

side up, and deep-fry 10-15 minutes, or until batter is golden and eggplant is soft.

To serve, arrange on lettuce leaves on individual plates and garnish as desired. **Serves 4 as an appetiser, 2 as a main dish.**

SOYA BEAN DIP
Nam Prik Tao Cheo Lon

Dips such as this one form the spicy part of many a meal, especially in the Northern capital of Chiang Mai. Northerners like to eat spicy dips with plates of raw and lightly steamed vegetables and a bowl or basket of sticky rice.

To eat this in Northern style, take a bite-sized ball of sticky rice in your fingers, squeeze it into whatever shape you prefer, dip into the nam prik and pop into your mouth.

As you can imagine, nam prik dips make great picnic items!

1 cup	coconut cream	250 mL
2 tbsp	ground pork	30 mL
1/2 cup	fermented soya beans	125 mL
2 tbsp	chopped shallots	30 mL
	A few slices of lemon grass	
1	wild lime (makrood) leaf, finely chopped	1
1 tsp	fructose (or other sweetener)	5 mL
3	fresh chillies, seeded and sliced	3

Bring 2 tbsp (30 mL) of the coconut cream slowly to the boil in a saucepan over gentle heat. Add the ground pork, cook, stirring, until pork is no longer pink, about 2 minutes.

Stir in remaining coconut cream, fermented soya beans, shallots, lemon grass and wild lime leaf. Season with fructose, then add the sliced chillies. Simmer on low heat for 5 minutes. Do not allow mixture to boil as it will cause the coconut oil to separate.

Serve at room temperature with fresh vegetables, either raw or very lightly steamed, and a bowl of sticky rice. Makes 1 cup (250 mL), enough for hors d'oeuvres for about 10.

Bruise lemon grass well before slicing. This will help to release the flavours.

TASTE
SWEET
SALTY

NORTHERN-STYLE GRILLED VEGETABLE RELISH
Nam Prik Nuum

This delightful dish from the north of Thailand has a hot and smoky barbecued flavour and is traditionally served with sticky rice and a platter of lightly steamed vegetables.

We've discovered it makes a wonderful accompaniment to all barbecued meats, especially lamb!

2	large garlic heads	2
6	shallots, unpeeled	6
15	finger-hot chillies	15
10	banana peppers	10
10	tiny bird chillies, or to taste	10
1	sweet red pepper	1
1	sweet yellow (or orange) pepper	1
1	small onion	1
1	small eggplant	1
3 tbsp	fish sauce	45 mL
3 tbsp plus 1 tsp	lime juice	50 mL
1 tsp	fructose	5 mL

On grill, place garlic, shallots, finger-hot chillies, hot banana peppers, tiny bird chillies, sweet red pepper, sweet yellow pepper, onion and eggplant; barbecue until cooked and the skins char and blister in places.

If desired, peel vegetable skins. Cut all vegetables into chunks and starting with the garlic, pound all together in a mortar and pestle, adding a few pieces at a time until relish is roughly blended. Vegetables will remain chunky but broken down enough to allow flavours to blend. Season with fish sauce, lime juice and fructose and serve at room temperature. **Makes about 1 1/2 cups (375 mL), or 4-6 servings.**

TASTE

HOT

SON-IN-LAW EGGS
Khaay Luuk Khooey

This dish is designed to give your taste buds a real Thai workout: it's sweet, sour, salty, hot and slightly bitter all at the same time.

The name in Thai is a play on the word *luuk*, which can mean eggs or any round object, depending upon context. I'll leave the interpretation to your imagination!

4-6	hard-boiled eggs	4-6
1 cup	light vegetable oil	250 mL
3	shallots	3
4 tbsp	palm sugar	60 mL
2-4 tbsp	fish sauce, to taste	30-60 mL
4 tbsp	tamarind puree	60 mL
4	sprigs fresh coriander	4
8-12	tiny red bird chillies	8-12

Peel hard-boiled eggs and cut in half. Heat oil in a wok and deep-fry the egg halves until the outsides are golden and blistered. Remove eggs with a slotted spoon and drain, flat side up, on paper towels.

Slice shallots and deep-fry in the hot oil until just golden. Remove with slotted spoon and drain on a paper towel.

Drain off most of the oil in wok, leaving about 2 tbsp (30 mL). Return to a medium-high heat, add palm sugar and cook, stirring vigorously, until sugar is melted. Add fish sauce and tamarind puree, bring to the boil. Reduce heat slightly and boil gently 5 minutes, stirring occasionally, or until sauce is thick, brown and slightly sticky. Taste and adjust seasoning.

Arrange the egg halves on a platter, yolk facing upward, and drizzle the sauce over them. Garnish with coriander, chillies and fried shallot. **Serves 4.**

TASTE

SWEET
SOUR
SALTY
HOT

STIR-FRIED CORN WITH BASIL
Khaopote Phad Baay Krapao

*The key
to the success of
this dish is to
cook it just
enough to warm
it through. In
the centre, the
corn kernels
should be sweet
and crunchy
and milky.*

*If you make
this dish very
mild, or without
any chillies,
add 1/2 tsp
(2 mL) pepper.*

Basil and corn are plentiful in late summer and early fall, which is an ideal time to serve this colourful dish. It tastes best when fresh sweet corn is used and is just lightly cooked, but you can make this at other times with frozen corn kernels or even with canned baby corn cobs.

3	small hot chillies	3
5	cloves garlic	5
2	fresh coriander roots	2
4 tsp	fish sauce	20 mL
20-30	fresh basil leaves	20-30
	Green and red chillies	
	(or sweet red peppers) to taste	
3 tbsp	vegetable oil	45 mL
2 cups	fresh corn kernels	500 mL
1 tsp	fructose (or other sweetener)	5 mL

Pound small hot chillies, garlic, coriander roots and 1 tsp (5 mL) fish sauce in a mortar to a coarse paste. Wash and dry basil leaves. Slice or julienne green and red chillies.

Heat a wok on high for 2 minutes. Add oil and stir-fry garlic paste 2 minutes, until aromatic. Add corn kernels and stir-fry 2 minutes. Stir in basil leaves, then add fructose, chillies and remaining fish sauce. Stir to mix, boil hard 1 minute. Turn onto serving dish and serve immediately. **Serves 4.**

TASTE
SWEET

STIR-FRIED BUTTERNUT SQUASH WITH EGG
Phad Fak Thong

This is a great dish for the fall when squash of all kinds start to appear.

Beware, though—some types of squash cook very quickly and tend to disintegrate when stir-fried. To see if a squash will hold up for stir-frying, test a small piece first by boiling. If it crumbles easily after being boiled for a few minutes, chances are it won't stand up to stir-frying. Use it for Sankhaya Fak Thong (see page 196) instead. For a spectacular presentation, serve in a hollowed-out or carved squash or pumpkin.

1 lb	butternut squash	500 g
2 tbsp	vegetable oil	30 mL
1	clove garlic, chopped	1
3.5 oz	thinly sliced pork loin	100 g
2	eggs, lightly beaten	2
2 tbsp	fish sauce	30 mL
1 1/2 tsp	fructose	7 mL

Peel squash and cut into chunks or slices. Blanch in a pot of rapidly boiling water 2-3 minutes, or until half cooked. Drain and set aside.

Heat oil in a wok. Add garlic and stir-fry briefly on high heat. Add pork and stir-fry 2 minutes or until meat turns white.

Add squash, stir-fry to mix. Add eggs, fish sauce and fructose and stir-fry until eggs are scrambled. Remove to a serving platter and serve hot. **Serves 4.**

TASTE
SWEET

8 GANGSTERS STIR-FRY
Phad 8 Sian

This dish calls for eight vegetables of the sprout type: tall, lean and green, white or yellow. Try it in the spring when fresh asparagus and fiddleheads hit the market.

At other times of the year, you can reduce your "gang" to five or six according to availability, or admit new members such as baby bok choy, beet greens or spinach.

6-10	canned bamboo shoots	6-10
1 cup	soya bean sprouts	250 mL
1 cup	mung bean sprouts	250 mL
10-15	stalks fresh asparagus	10-15
1	small bunch watercress (15-20 stalks)	1
1	small bunch Oriental water spinach (pak bung)	1
1/2 cup	fresh fiddleheads	125 mL
3 tbsp	light vegetable oil	45 mL
4	cloves garlic, chopped	4
1	small bunch (20 stalks) fresh chive flowers (in the bud stage)	1
2 tbsp	fish sauce	30 mL
2 tsp	fructose	10 mL
1 tsp	fermented soya beans	5 mL

Cut off any tough parts and trim bamboo shoots to roughly the same size. In a small pot, boil bamboo shoots in water to cover, about 10 minutes. Drain and discard cooking water.

Discard roots from both types of bean sprouts. Put bean sprouts in a bowl of ice water until ready to cook.

Wash asparagus, watercress, water spinach and fiddleheads. Cut or trim so that all pieces are, as far as possible, the same size, and keep in a bowl of ice water. Drain well before using.

Heat oil in a wok over high heat. Add garlic, stir-fry briefly. Add vegetables, starting with the ones that will take longest to cook. Allow the pan to come up to high heat each time before adding another batch of vegetables. Cook vegetables in this order: asparagus, bamboo shoots, fiddleheads, chive flowers, spinach, watercress, soya bean sprouts, mung bean sprouts.

Add fish sauce, fructose and fermented soya beans, stir-fry until well mixed. Turn onto a serving platter and serve immediately. **Serves 6.**

TASTE

SALTY

TONGUE-TICKLER STIR-FRY
Phad Prik Youack

In this electrifying dish, peppers leave the world of garnish and spice and become a vegetable.

If you're crazy, use some red finger-hot chillies as well and really go for it! And always remember—this dish is just *loaded* with Vitamin C!

12	yellow (or green) banana peppers	12
3.5 oz	pork (or beef) tenderloin	100 g
2 tbsp	light vegetable oil	30 mL
3	cloves garlic, minced	3
1 tbsp	fish sauce	15 mL
1 tbsp	oyster sauce	15 mL
1 tsp	fructose	5 mL
1 tsp	fermented soya beans	5 mL

Remove stems from banana peppers and slice lengthwise in 4 or 6 pieces. Slice meat very thinly in strips.

Heat oil in a wok over high heat. Stir-fry garlic briefly. Add pork strips and stir-fry 2 minutes. Add peppers and stir-fry 2 minutes.

Add fish sauce, oyster sauce, fructose and fermented soya beans; stir to mix. Cover and remove from heat. Allow to sit for 1 or 2 minutes, then turn onto a platter and serve. **Serves 2-4.**

TASTE
HOT

THAI GROUND PORK OMELETTE
Khaay Jiaw Muu Sap

This main course Thai omelette is an eat-anytime dish that goes especially well with Joke (see page 170) and Khaaw Tom (Midnight Soup) (see page 168). Serve this as a main course dish with thick soups, hot curries or hot yum salads.

A great favourite with small guests, the unique flavour depends on cooking the egg until it is crispy. The pork remains soft and the shallots will be a little undercooked.

Vary this by using any other chopped meat, fish or chopped tofu as desired.

4	eggs	4
5 oz	ground pork	150 g
2	large shallots, sliced	2
2	green onions, chopped	2
3 tbsp	fish sauce	45 mL
1/2 tsp	ground pepper, or to taste	2 mL
5 tbsp	vegetable oil	75 mL

In a bowl, combine eggs, pork, shallots, green onions, fish sauce and pepper and mix well.

Heat oil in a wok. Pour in half the egg mixture and spread it evenly over the pan, about 1 1/4 inches (3 cm) thick.

Cook on high about 2-3 minutes, until egg sets and bubbles. Turn over—you can break it into several pieces—and continue cooking on high or medium-high until egg is crispy and almost burnt. Repeat with second half of the mixture. Serves 2.

TASTE
SALTY

CRUNCHY EGGPLANT STIR-FRY
Phad Makua Yaaw

The Bangkok Garden team developed this for our vegetarian menu. Very strict vegetarians can substitute salt for fish sauce.

We love the contrast of the soft eggplant and the crisp water chestnuts.

3	long eggplants	3
1 cup	drained canned water chestnuts	250 mL
3 tbsp	vegetable oil	45 mL
1 tsp	minced garlic	5 mL
1 tsp	fermented soya beans	5 mL
1 tbsp	fructose	15 mL
2 tbsp	fish sauce	30 mL
	Fresh Thai basil leaves	
4 tbsp	sweet (or hot) red pepper chunks	60 mL

Soak eggplants 1 hour in cold water. Trim and cut into bite-sized pieces. Steam 10 minutes to soften. Cut water chestnuts into matchstick pieces.

Heat oil in a wok over high heat. Add garlic, stir-fry briefly, then add soya beans and stir until mixed. Add eggplant and stir to mix. Add fructose, fish sauce and water chestnuts; stir-fry 5 minutes. Taste and adjust seasoning if necessary.

Add basil leaves and peppers, stir briefly. Turn onto a serving platter and serve. **Serves 4.**

Steaming will ensure the eggplants maintain their colour. If you stir-fry them raw, the skins will turn black.

TASTE
SWEET
SALTY

CHAPTER 12
DESSERTS

I am often asked why we don't serve more Thai desserts at Bangkok Garden.

The truth is, traditional Thai desserts are so different that most Westerners don't like them on first taste and no matter how much they like the rest of the Thai menu, never acquire a taste for Thai sweets.

A Thai meal as a matter of course ends with fresh fruit, to cleanse the palate and alert the taste buds that the sensory onslaught is over. A formal Thai meal will end with two kinds of dessert, one liquid and one solid, in addition to the fresh fruit.

The desserts are concocted from a very few simple ingredients: flours of sticky rice, tapioca and mung bean, eggs, sugar, coconut milk, agar-agar and tropical flavours such as rose, jasmine, pandanus and citrus. "Cakes" are generally made of sweetened sticky rice mixed with some flavourings and pressed to a solid form. Jellies are made with agar-agar, a seaweed extract that does not break down in the heat like gelatine. They are then flavoured with essences and perhaps topped with sweet and slightly salty coconut cream.

Some liquid desserts consist of fruits (or possibly kidney or mung beans or taro root) cooked in a sugar syrup, then served in a bowl with coconut cream and crushed ice. Others are made of rice, tapioca or mung bean flour batters forced through molds into various shapes, poached in sugar syrup and served with coconut cream and crushed ice.

As simple as the recipes sound, many of these desserts are not all that easy to make, and many Thais never bother to master the art of sweet-making, preferring to purchase sweets when necessary at the market. American and European-style cakes are also popular, with countless bakeries in Bangkok and other cities producing fine-quality products.

In preparing to cook these desserts, it is important to obtain the right flours. Please read the section on flours in Chapter 2, and make sure you have the right one for the job. Otherwise, your recipe may fall apart in the middle of the cooking process!

If you're really going all out to make these special desserts, it's worth taking the extra time to make the coconut milk from scratch (see page 100), rather than opening a can. You'll notice a big difference in the taste when the coconut isn't fighting 15 to 20 other ingredients for your attention, as it might in a curry.

And finally, if you don't like the sound of any of these classic Thai desserts, or lack the time to practise them before your dinner party, don't hesitate to do what any Thai hostess at a smart Bangkok party would do—buy or bake your favourite European or American-style cake and serve it with pride.

COCONUT PUMPKIN CUSTARD
Sankhaya Fak Thong

This dish can be a real culinary tour de force if you incise the pumpkin skin with a design before you cook it. If you're not up to major sculpture, scallop the rim of the pumpkin and bring the dessert to the table whole for dramatic effect.

In the markets of Thailand, sweet makers bake this custard in huge trays and sprinkle matchsticks of pumpkin on top. It's sold cut into small cubes. You can do this at home as well if you want to serve smaller portions.

At Bangkok Garden, we serve a selection of Thai desserts cut into bite-sized morsels along with several pieces of seasonal fresh fruit. This gives guests a taste of several things without committing to a large portion of something unknown.

3	eggs	3
5 tbsp	palm sugar	75 mL
3/4 cup	coconut cream	175 mL
1/4 tsp	rose water	1 mL
1	small pumpkin, about 1 1/2 times the size of a grapefruit	1

In a bowl, beat eggs lightly, add sugar and coconut cream, stirring until sugar dissolves. Add rose water.

Cut an opening in the top of the pumpkin and remove seeds and strings. Scrape with a spoon to leave inner surface smooth.

Pour egg mixture into pumpkin to come just to the top. Put the pumpkin in a dish that just fits it and put the dish in a steamer. Steam for 30-60 minutes or until a knife inserted deep into the custard's centre comes out clean. Cool to room temperature, then chill in refrigerator.

To serve, cut into wedge-shaped slices so each serving is a portion of custard surrounded by pumpkin. If you like, run a knife around the edge of each slice to remove pumpkin skin. Serves 8.

At Bangkok Garden, we often use acorn squash or carved butternut squash.

TASTE

SWEET

STEAMED COCONUT CUSTARD
Sankhaya

This simple Thai sweet falls somewhere between custard and the squares or bars we are familiar with in North America. It is traditionally served cut into small squares: it's so thick and rich, one piece may be enough.

Thais like to top these custard squares with a variety of oddball garnishes, including toasted sesame seeds, deep-fried shallot slices and even dried shrimp.

3	eggs	3
5 tbsp	palm sugar	75 mL
3/4 cup	coconut cream	175 mL
1/4 tsp	rose water or pandanus extract	1 mL
4 tbsp	grated or shredded coconut	60 mL
4 tbsp	toasted coconut, for garnish	60 mL
	Fresh fruit	

In a bowl, beat eggs lightly, add sugar and coconut cream, stirring until sugar dissolves. Add rose water.

If using dried coconut, soak it first in a little milk or water for 10 minutes or until liquid is absorbed; otherwise it will absorb too much coconut milk during the cooking process, and your custard will be too dry.

Combine egg mixture with grated coconut, pour into a glass dish (mixture should be about "2 fingers" deep) and cover. Steam on top of the stove in an Oriental steamer, or place dish in a shallow pan of boiling water (bain marie) and bake in 350°F (180°C) oven for approximately 1 hour, or until a knife inserted into the centre of the custard comes out clean.

Chill thoroughly. Cut into small squares, garnish with toasted coconut, and serve with fresh fruit. **Makes about 25 squares.**

TASTE
SWEET

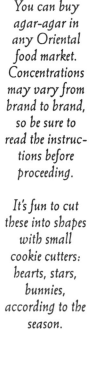

SWEET
SALTY

TROPICAL JELLIES
Woon Naa Gati

These jellies don't wiggle and wobble like traditional North American desserts because they're made with agar-agar, a seaweed product that does not break down at room temperature the way gelatin does. This is especially important in the intense heat of tropical Thailand.

These tropical jellies come in two layers: a clear shimmering jelly tinted and flavoured in your favourite way, and a pure white sweet-salty coconut cream layer on top. As an added bonus, these jellies are safe to serve to your vegetarian guests!

Thais like their desserts very sweet. I have adjusted these to be lightly refreshing to Western palates. By all means play around with the quantities until you find the sweetness that suits you.

CLEAR JASMINE JELLY

1 cup	boiling water	250 mL
1	package agar-agar	1
4 tbsp	fructose (or other sweetener)	60 mL
	Few drops red food colouring	
	Few drops jasmine essence	

CLEAR PANDANUS JELLY

1 cup	boiling water	250 mL
1	package agar-agar	1
4 tbsp	fructose (or other sweetener)	60 mL
	Few drops green food colouring	
	Few drops pandanus flavouring	

COCONUT CREAM TOPPING

1	package agar-agar	1
1 tbsp	hot water	15 mL
1 cup	coconut cream	250 mL
2 tbsp	fructose (or other sweetener)	30 mL
1 tsp	salt	5 mL

Clear Jasmine Jelly: Pour boiling water over the agar-agar and stir until dissolved. Add fructose and stir until dissolved. Add red food colouring and jasmine essence, mix well. Pour into a glass mold or dish. The jelly should be at least 2 fingers deep. Refrigerate until set.

Clear Pandanus Jelly: Repeat process as for jasmine jelly.

Coconut Cream Topping: Dissolve agar-agar in hot water. Stir into the coconut cream. Add fructose and salt, and pour half over each clear jelly. Refrigerate until thoroughly set. Cut into shapes and serve with slices of fresh fruit.

TARO BALLS IN COCONUT CREAM
Bua Loi Puak

A thick, rich dessert, this should be served warm or at room temperature in very small bowls.

   This can be made ahead and reheated just before serving. Make sure you don't allow the coconut milk to boil, though, or the coconut oil will begin to separate out and make your dessert look oily.

2 cups	sticky rice flour	500 mL
1 cup	cornstarch	250 mL
6-8 tbsp	water	90-120 mL
1 cup	mashed cooked taro	250 mL
1 cup	palm sugar	250 mL
4 cups	coconut milk	1 L

Combine sticky rice flour and cornstarch in a mixing bowl. Stir in water, a little at a time. Gradually add mashed taro and mix with a pastry-cutter until you can knead the mixture. Knead until thoroughly mixed. Roll into balls about the size of large marbles, and set aside.

   In large saucepan, dissolve the palm sugar in the coconut milk over low heat, stirring constantly. Bring to the boil and add the taro balls; return to the boil. Reduce heat to a high simmer and cook gently for 10 minutes, stirring occasionally to prevent balls from sticking to each other. (You may have to do this job in several batches, according to the size of your pot.)

   Serve hot or warm in small bowls with about a dozen taro balls and 5 tbsp (75 mL) of the coconut cooking liquid. Serves 10.

TASTE
SWEET

*The dish
is a Thai
adaptation of
an 18th century
Portuguese
sweetmeat.*

MOCK JACK-FRUIT SEEDS
Met Khanoon

The jack-fruit is enormous, with a hard, prickly dusty-green exterior. Inside in several compartments are dozens of yellow "fruits" surrounding large black seeds.

These mock jack-fruit are constructed of a marzipan-like dough, coated in sweetened egg yolk for the yellow covering, and cooked in a sugar syrup.

2 cups	mung beans	500 mL
1 cup	coconut cream	250 mL
7 cups	granulated sugar	1.75 L
6 cups	water	1.5 L
12	egg yolks, lightly beaten	12

Soak mung beans overnight in a large basin of cold water. In the morning the skins should be loose and many will be floating on the water. Skim these off with a slotted spoon. Agitate the beans and remove any more skins that come loose.

Transfer the mung beans to a bowl or the top half of a steamer pot, removing any skins that remain. Steam beans 30 minutes, or until soft. Mash with a potato masher until smooth.

Put the paste in the top of a double boiler. Blend in the coconut cream and 3 cups (750 mL) sugar. Cook, stirring and mashing with a wooden spoon until sugar melts and the mixture forms a stiff paste. Remove from heat and set aside to cool. Roll into small oblong shapes like jack-fruit seeds. Set aside.

Put the remaining 4 cups (1 L) sugar and water in a saucepan. Boil the syrup gently over a medium heat for 30 minutes, until slightly thickened. Set aside half of the syrup and chill.

Bring the remaining syrup in the saucepan to the boil. Dip the mock jack-fruit seeds in the beaten egg yolks and then slide them into the boiling syrup. Cook until the egg yolk coating is firm and set, about 4 minutes. Remove with a slotted spoon and put them in the bowl of cool syrup to prevent them from sticking together.

When ready to serve, drain and arrange on a serving plate. May be served hot, cold or at room temperature. **Makes approximately 20 mock jack-fruit seeds. Most people will eat 1 or 2, as they are rich.**

T
A
S
T
E

SWEET

MOCK POMEGRANATE SEEDS
Tupthim Grob

Thais love a culinary joke, and this one looks exactly like the real thing. The crunchy water chestnut "seed" surrounded by the soft ruby tapioca "flesh" is guaranteed to surprise and delight your guests. Of course, it's not refreshingly tart like fresh pomegranate seeds, but enjoy it for the crunch of the water chestnut playing off against the crunch of the crushed ice, and the silky smoothness of the tapioca coating echoing the smoothness of the coconut milk.

As an added bonus, this is probably the easiest of the Thai desserts to make.

Thais tend to like these desserts very sweet; I suggest you adjust the sweetness to suit your own palate.

1 cup	diced water chestnuts	250 mL
	Few drops red food colouring	
1 cup	tapioca flour	250 mL
1 cup	granulated sugar	250 mL
4 tbsp	water	60 mL
	Few drops jasmine or pandanus flavour if desired	
1 cup	coconut milk	250 mL
	Crushed ice	

In a bowl, sprinkle the water chestnuts with a few drops of red colouring; mix well. Add the tapioca flour and shake until the chestnuts are well coated.

Bring 4 cups (1 L) water to the boil in a medium saucepan and pour in the coated water chestnuts, stirring just enough to prevent sticking. When they float and the flour coating turns to a clear jelly, remove with a slotted spoon to a bowl of cold water. Allow to cool for a few minutes, then drain and set aside.

In a saucepan, dissolve the sugar in 4 tbsp (60 mL) water over a low heat. Bring to a boil and remove from the heat to cool; add flavour if desired.

Serve mock pomegranate seeds in individual glass bowls together with equal quantities (about 4 tbsp/60 mL) each of sugar syrup, coconut milk and crushed ice. **Serves 4-6.**

The Thai penchant for making charming look-alikes originates from the Royal Household, whose artistic cooks make a habit of turning quite ordinary ingredients into a visual and taste sensation.

TASTE
SWEET

If you do not have a heavy saucepan, use a double boiler.

If you can't get mangoes, try this dessert with a favourite fruit in season: peaches, strawberries, raspberries or whatever takes your fancy.

MANGOES AND STICKY RICE
Khaaw Niaw Mamuang

From blossom to harvest, the subject of the year's mango crop is always a hot topic. When the blossoms first appear on the tall graceful mango trees in February, everyone waits anxiously for the mango blossom rains, gentle afternoon showers that help to pollinate and "set" the fruit.

As they form, the number and size of fruits are assessed by expert eyes. It is a great relief to those awaiting the mango harvest when a satisfactory number of fruits appear on the stems hanging all over the trees like so many ornaments.

As harvest time approaches, people start dreaming of their favourite varieties—there are a dozen or more, each with its own characteristic flavour. Some are sweet and perfume-y, others are tart and still others almost resinous. Some are eaten green, dipped in a mixture of salt, sugar and chilli peppers, or in a sugar syrup laced with fried shallots and toasted chillies.

When the sweet juicy mangoes are ready for harvest, about mid-May, sweet sellers in the markets begin to prepare for their busiest season.

As the season progresses, different varieties of mango come into season and it's not unusual for enthusiasts to wax poetic on the subject of their favourites.

In Thailand, the mango season is over by the end of June (that's when the durian and rambutan enthusiasts are starting to get cranked up) but in North America we can generally find mangoes imported from somewhere almost all the time.

2 cups	sticky rice, soaked overnight and drained	500 mL
1 cup	coconut cream	250 mL
1/2 cup	fructose (or other sweetener)	125 mL
1 tsp	salt	5 mL
6	ripe mangoes, peeled and sliced	6
2 tbsp	toasted sesame seeds (optional)	30 mL

Wrap sticky rice in a clean tea towel and steam for 30 minutes, until grains are firm but no longer hard inside.

In a small heavy-bottomed saucepan over low heat, combine coconut cream, fructose and salt, stirring until fructose has dissolved. Do not allow coconut cream to boil, as the coconut oil will begin to separate from the cream. Remove from heat. Reserve and chill 4 tbsp (60 mL) of the cream.

TASTE
SWEET

Put cooked sticky rice in a bowl and pour remaining warm coconut cream over. Using a couple of large forks, toss gently together until well blended. Serve hot, warm or room temperature in individual portions or mounded on a serving dish. Arrange mango slices around sticky rice, spoon chilled coconut cream over top and garnish (if desired) with toasted sesame seeds. Serves 4-6.

THAI FRIED BANANAS
Kluay Tod

Thai banana fritters have a very thin, crispy batter. The shredded coconut is almost a secret ingredient. The success of the dish depends on using firm bananas. Ripe ones will produce a sweet but soggy fritter.

1 cup	rice flour	250 mL
1/2 cup	all-purpose wheat flour	125 mL
1/2 tsp	salt	2 mL
3/4 tsp	baking powder	4 mL
2 tbsp	palm sugar	30 mL
3/4 cup	water or coconut milk	175 mL
1 cup	shredded coconut	250 mL
8	very firm bananas	8
2 1/2 cups	light vegetable oil for deep-frying	625 mL
2 tbsp	toasted sesame seeds, for garnish	30 mL

In bowl, combine flours, salt, baking powder and palm sugar and mix well. Add water or coconut milk and mix to the consistency of thick cream. Stir in shredded coconut.

Cut bananas in half lengthwise, then widthwise to produce 4 pieces.

In wok, heat oil gently over moderate heat 10 minutes. Dip banana pieces in batter, allowing most of the batter to run off. Slide into hot oil and fry 3-4 minutes, until golden brown.

Remove, drain, arrange on a platter and sprinkle with toasted sesame seeds.

Serve hot or warm. **Serves 8.**

If you like a very sweet dish, drizzle some warm honey over the fritters before serving. Don't let them sit around or they'll go soggy on you.

SWEET

INDEX